The politics of participation

MANCHESTER
1824

Manchester University Press

The politics of participation

From Athens to e-democracy

Matt Qvortrup

Manchester University Press

The right of Matt Qvortrup to be identified as the author of this work has been asserted by him in accordance with the Copyright, Designs and Patents Act 1988.

Published by Manchester University Press
Altrincham Street, Manchester M1 7JA, UK
www.manchesteruniversitypress.co.uk

British Library Cataloguing-in-Publication Data is available

Library of Congress Cataloging-in-Publication Data is available

ISBN 978 0 7190 7659 6 *paperback*

First published by Manchester University Press 2007

This edition first published 2016

The publisher has no responsibility for the persistence or accuracy of URLs for any external or third-party internet websites referred to in this book, and does not guarantee that any content on such websites is, or will remain, accurate or appropriate.

Printed by Lightning Source

But I, my life surveying,
With nothing to show, to devise, from its idle years
Nor houses, nor lands – nor tokens of gems or gold for my friends,
Only these Souvenirs of Democracy –
In them – in all my songs – behind me leaving.

(Walt Whitman, *Souvenirs of Democracy*)

Contents

List of illustrations

Boxes

Figure

Tables

Acknowledgements

This book could not have been written without the help of Peter McLaverty, Pippa Norris, Richard Jenkins, Nigel Smith, Dahlia Scheindlin, Gary Sussman, Rick Ridder, Quintin Oliver, Tony Wright, Robert Smith, Laurence Morel, Oonagh Gay, Elizabeth Tait, Michael Saward, Clive Bean, Neil Kenlock, David Sanders, Iain MacLeod, Allan McConnell, Darren Halpin, Anne Van Ewyk, Mark Rolfe, Bjørn Erik Rasch, Ethan Putterman, Patricia Springborg, Lyn Carson, Ted Becker, Alistair Anderson, Ed Page, Joop van Holsteyn, Patrick Dumont and Deborah Brennan. I am grateful also to the Robert Gordon University for sponsoring the sabbatical during which much of this book was written, and to the universities of Sydney and New South Wales for their hospitality during my sojourn in Australia. The Economic and Social Research Council is acknowledged for granting me a fellowship in 2006 to pursue the ideas covered in chapter 4. Lastly I owe special thanks to Anne Bamford for being so generous, kind and wise. This book is dedicated to my sons Sebastian and Frederik with love!

Lisbon, 12 March 2006

A note on the data

Material in chapters 3–6 is based on analyses of *Eurobarometer*, European Values Surveys and secondary analyses of the *British Election Survey*. The analysis in chapter 10 is based on participant observation in the Netherlands and France in the spring and summer of 2005 and on opinion polls conducted in the native languages of the two countries. In France it is based on IPSOS, carried out 29 May 2005; in the Netherlands the data is based on three TweeVandaag Opinion Panle (Opinion Polls) carried out on 5 April 2005 ($N = 15283$), 9 May 2005 ($N = 13459$), and 28 May 2005 ($N = 17195$). For Luxembourg the data are based on opinion polls carried out for the main national newspaper *Lëtzebuerger* by ILReS Market Research throughout the first six months of 2005.

Introduction

In human societies collective decisions can be reached as a result of three different mechanisms (or combinations thereof): by talking, by voting or by fighting.

The politics of participation involves all three forms. We endorse talking and voting because they are activities based on peaceful and reasoned arguments, and we condemn violence because we know that might is not right. The ideal is peaceable decision-making, but as sociologists and political scientists we must acknowledge that occasionally – if options are limited – people resort to violence – even in democratic societies. It is not only among states that 'war is the continuation of politics by other means', as Clausewitz famously observed in *On War*.

This book is devoted to an analysis of talking, voting and fighting among citizens, in an attempt to understand why and when ordinary people engage in these activities or combinations of them.

It might be a good idea to consider initially a simple statistic about the United Kingdom: the National Trust has 2.5 million members and the Royal Society for the Protection of Birds has 1.04 million members. Far from suggesting that birds and stately homes are unimportant, it might be a reason for concern that either organisation has many more members than the three main political parties put together. Labour has 361,000 paid-up members, the Conservatives 350,000 and the Liberal Democrats 90,000 (Walker 2001). Do these figures suggest that we have become disengaged, that we care less and less about politics? Is British democracy in a state of crisis? Research by American writers Almond and Verba in the early 1960s showed that Britain had a model civic culture characterised by a high level of citizen participation and strong civic norms that fostered political stability and effective policy-making (Almond and Verba 1963). The general consensus in the press in recent years has been the opposite.

No political phenomenon can be analysed without a firm understanding of method, and this is especially true for citizen politics.

Political activity defies traditional boundaries. Sometimes political activists use arguments, at other times they vote – and occasionally they resort to violence; in other words: talking, voting and fighting. To understand political action we are required to have an open mind and to be open to different methods.

In chapter 1 an account is developed of what is required for the study of political phenomena. Using a largely qualitative method, drawing on writers like C. Wright Mills, Richard Fenno, Clifford Geertz and above all Hannah Arendt, it is argued that political participation cannot be understood from an objective perspective only, and that one needs to study the phenomenon *from the inside*. Quantitative approaches certainly have a place in the study of politics, but a *full* understanding of the phenomenon is possible only if we combine different approaches, seeking – like detectives – to patch together the story. Consequently, an understanding of citizen politics requires that we adopt the perspective of the citizens in question and take seriously their grievances and concerns. To do so we must transcend – but not abandon – the idea that politics can be adequately studied objectively; we must combine the various perspectives of what has been called the 'sociological imagination' (Mills 2002). Chapter 1 presents a *tour de force* of the argument and the rationale behind this way of analysing politics.

Having outlined an overall approach to studying citizen politics, I turn in chapter 2 to historical debates about citizen politics. Throughout the history of civilised society, citizen politics has been the exception rather than the norm. Most societies through the ages have been based not on citizen engagement but on more or less despotic rule. Why, then, should citizens be involved in politics and, indeed, take a direct part in the process of governing? An answer to this question requires an understanding of the development of the philosophical debates about citizen participation through the ages. Beginning with the Greek philosophers Plato and Aristotle, the chapter presents a general account of the defence of citizen politics provided by Machiavelli and Marsilius of Padua, Rousseau and Mill, but also an introduction to the elitist critics of democracy, e.g. José Ortega y Gasset and the federalists. Following this general overview, more contemporary theorists are introduced.

In Part II I consider the issues empirically. Comprised of a number of smaller sections (or sub-chapters), chapter 3 centres around the central issues concerning citizen politics. Adopting an empirical approach, I present a typology of different forms of citizen politics, from activities initiated by the people themselves to actions prompted by the elites; similarly, citizen politics can be divided into *conservative* or *progressive* effects. Based on this typology, different forms of politics are analysed.

In the remaining chapters of Part II, the four categories are analysed in turn and explanations developed as to the causes and determinants behind different kinds of political action, whether elite-driven or citizen-initiated.

Chapter 4 considers the 'illegal' – but not necessarily illegitimate – aspects of citizen politics, including terrorism, while chapter 5 focuses on novel means of political engagement that have emerged in recent years (including teledemocracy and the internet, and deliberative democracy, the political parties' use of designer politics and political marketing). I argue that the increased use of political consultants can in some cases strengthen democratic legitimacy by ensuring that citizens' preferences are acknowledged in policies.

Having considered various aspects of direct engagement I turn in chapter 6 to consider theories of electoral choice in an attempt to explain why people vote and what determines their preferences; the chapter considers also the influence of the mass media.

Chapter 7 is an excursus on the UK Parliament. It is often argued that politics should be left to (elected) experts and that Parliament is the proper forum for democratic deliberation. The question is, however, whether that is an accurate description of the reality of Parliament. To answer this question we consider the procedures and powers of the UK Parliament.

Part III looks at practical citizen politics in the form of three case studies of referendums and citizen politics. While support for increased participation is a constant theme in the political rhetoric of the elites, decisions to submit more issues to the voters do not always live up to their idealistic billing.

The decision to hold referendums is a case in point, and chapter 8 considers why governments have submitted issues to referendums (both in the UK and elsewhere). Chapter 9's concern, citizenship engagement, is pursued through a case study of the 2005 referendums on the European Constitution in Spain, France, the Netherlands and Luxembourg, while chapter 10 considers the effects of postal voting (one of the favoured options for increasing participation). Together these three case studies present an overview of the state of democracy in Western democracies as well as touching on some of the possible means of (re-)engaging citizens with the political process.

The book concludes with a discussion of democracy's prospects, in the course of which I sum up the argument, make recommendations for future studies and offer suggestions for new forms of participation.

Contrary to the often negative assessment of the state of citizen engagement, I contend that if citizen politics is to thrive a broadening of the political system itself is required to allow for different forms of democratic participation.

Part I

Theoretical aspects of citizen politics

Democracy is what social scientists call a social construct. It is not a phenomenon which can be studied experimentally or in the way that phenomena are studied by the natural sciences. What then is democracy?

In chapter 1 I consider some of the problems involved in the study of so loosely defined a concept and phenomenon as 'democracy' in terms of the methods of political science. After a critical introduction to the subject – and a critique of the idea that popular government can be analysed in a *scientific* manner – I turn to an alternative, more humanist, approach to the study of politics.

As a social construct itself, politics has a history, and in one sense the debate about democracy is a dialogue with more than 2000 years of ongoing discussions of the subject. Chapter 2 presents an account of the history of citizen democracy, from ancient Greece to the present day, with an emphasis on political and philosophical ideas.

1

Understanding citizen politics: a methodological overview

Before beginning this analysis of the problems of political participation, it is necessary to briefly consider how we might study a phenomenon as complex and multifaceted as politics.

There is no simple answer to that question. David Hume, the eighteenth-century Scottish philosopher, inspired by Isaac Newton, suggested that '[p]olitics may be reduced to a science' (Hume 1985), yet he failed to spell out what, if any, laws of politics obtained in his discipline. Political scientists of subsequent centuries, it seems, have not had much luck in their similar endeavours. Laws such as Robert Michels's 'iron law of oligarchy' (Michels 1911) and Duverger's 'Law' (according to which first-past-the-post electoral systems lead to two-party systems) are either trivially true (in the case of Michels) or have been falsified by actual events – thus, that Canada has more than two main parties falsifies Duverger's 'Law', if it was intended to be a *law* in the first place. Indeed, it might be argued that the search for such 'laws' is altogether misplaced – and is even obsolete in the sciences themselves. As Hannah Arendt (1983, 61) has put it, the concept of laws in the social sciences and history was

> always a metaphor borrowed from nature; and the fact is that this metaphor no longer convinces us because it has turned out that natural science can by no means be sure of an unchallengeable rule of law in nature.

Those who (still) entertain the thought that politics can – in due course – become a *science* are seemingly forced to agree with Karl Popper's observation that politics is 'yet to find its Newton or Galileo' (1957, 1).

Keeping within scientific discourse, the science of politics (if it can be thus called), is characterised by being in a constant state of flux, with its competing paradigms, epistemologies and theoretical approaches. Political science, to use the terminology of philosopher of science Thomas S. Kuhn, is in a revolutionary period (see Polsby 1998, 199). According to Kuhn scientific disciplines can be divided into two phases: a *revolutionary* phase, where competing schools battle over the proper study of the discipline; and a *normal* phase, where there is universal agreement on an established paradigm and most work in the scholarly community is guided towards puzzle-solving, i.e. fitting in the last pieces of the jigsaw to establish a complete picture (1962, 36). During periods of *normal* science, the process of scholarly discovery is cumulative. And, while political science may not have made discoveries on a par with those of Kepler, Newton or Boyle, some argue that political science *has* made progress and that it has now established a 'paradigm'.

Presenting a case for rational-choice theory – often defined as the use of micro-economic models in the study of politics –Shepsle and Bonchek have argued that political science may not yet be 'rocket science', but the use of sophisticated mathematical models means that politics can be studied using some of the same models that are applied by astrophysicists and chemists. As they put it:

> The transformation of the study of politics from storytelling and anecdote swapping, first to thick description and history writing, then to systematic measurement, and more recently to explanation and analysis, constitutes a significant movement along the scientific trajectory (1997, 7).

Arguing in a similar vein, Almond (1996, 50–51) has opined:

> If we were to model the history of political science in the form of a curve of scientific progress in the study of politics over the ages, it would probably begin in Greek political science, make some modest progress in the Roman centuries, not make much progress in the Middle Ages, rise a bit in the Renaissance and the Enlightenment, make some substantial gains in the 19th century, and then take off in solid growth in the 20th century . . . It [political science] is 'progressive' in the sense that it imputes the notion of improvement to the history of political studies, in the quantity of knowledge, and in quality in terms of both insight and rigor. With respect to insight, most colleagues would agree that Michael Waltzer (1983) has a better grasp of the concept of justice than does Plato, and with respect to rigor (and insight as well) Robert Dahl (1989) gives us a better theory of democracy than did Aristotle.

But can this view be justified? The view that Waltzer and Dahl knew more about justice and democracy than, respectively, Plato and Aristotle seems questionable, and is perhaps best repudiated by the prediction that more people in 200 years time will read Plato and Aristotle than Dahl and Waltzer.

The problem with Almond's statement is that it assumes that in political science theoretical debates can be concluded with finality. This has not been the case in the past. Whereas theoretical physicists would waste time by delving into the finer points of Johannes Kepler and Tycho Brahe's writings, and are well advised to concentrate on the most recent research, the reverse is true for political scientists. It is impossible to understand the debate about the politics of participation without being familiar with the great debates from Plato and onwards. Politics – like the arts – never takes place in a vacuum, is always historically conditioned, and constantly refers back to previous experiences and practices (see chapter 2).

Even if we focus on the empirical side of Almond's argument it seems that he has a rather weak case with regard to what politics – *qua* a science – has in fact accomplished. In the 1960s, so-called structural functionalists and behaviourists (of which Almond was one) believed that various models of cybernetics and applied sociology provided insights on the political process that answered the fundamental questions. Today, these models are sometimes invoked, though they are not treated as veridical.

More recently, rational-choice theorists have developed theories that purport to demonstrate the possibility of predicting the outcome of elections using the models of economic forecasting (Lewis-Beck and Rice 1990). The problem with these models is twofold: they have been empirically falsified; and they are based on a relatively short period in time. The main objection against scientific models is, however, that they are based on an idea of unchangeable individuals. Homo sapiens – a species of individuals possessed of free will – do not conform to the rigid models of mathematics. This is not a novel insight – though it is an important one. Adam Smith rejected this idea of 'the man of the system' who seems to

> imagine that he can arrange the different members of a great society with as much ease as the hand that arranges the different pieces upon a chessboard. He [the man of the system] does not consider that the pieces upon the chess board have no other principle of motion besides that which the hand impresses upon them; but that in the great chess-board of human society, every single piece has a principle of motion of its own, altogether different from that which the legislature might choose to impress upon it. (2002, 275)

To be sure, such problems might – conceivably – be remedied by using so-called dynamic mathematical models (Cooper 2004). Yet, while such models might be accurate, it is questionable that they reveal much about the actual motivations of the actors, in a way that is useful both to citizens and to practitioners.

Given that there is no paradigm of politics – and that such a paradigm seems to be an epistemological impossibility (cf. Smith's discussion of the man of the system) – an alternative model needs to be developed.

The model proposed here is based on the premiss that we want to *understand* the political agents, i.e. why citizens get involved in participatory democracy. The fundamental assumption is this: politics is a cultural activity, which changes in response to numerous personal, social and cultural factors. To fully grasp the nature and significance of political events and phenomena, we must steep ourselves in the details in a process of what cultural anthropologist Clifford Geertz has called 'thick description'. That political phenomenon is 'something to which social events, behaviours, institutions, or processes can be causally attributed; it is a context, something within which they can be intelligibly – that is thickly – described' (Geertz 1973, 14).

While the mathematical models might capture quantitative aspects of the political process – and are useful and interesting in that respect – they do not provide us with the full overview and with a deeper understanding. To understand the politics of participation (i.e. the subject of this book), it is certainly useful to consider statistical models and apply these (as will be done in chapters 3 and 4), but the use of quantitative models must always be a complement to an overall quest for a narrative grounded in cultural and practical developments. William James, the American pragmatist, made a case for this view suggesting that proper scholarly activity 'ekes out the narrowness of personal experience by concepts which it finds useful but not sovereign; but it stays inside the flux of life expectantly, recording facts, not formulating laws'. (James 1948, 98).

In the present book, the aim is not, therefore, to develop an overall theory – or paradigm – of political participation, but rather to bring together different aspects of the phenomenon, which will be defined as 'the politics of participation' by bringing together different facts and sources of information. As French political scientist Raymond Aron argued this is so because in the 'political order multiple causes determine events', that is, 'the destiny of a collectively is the result of multiple phenomena, external and internal to the group' (1994, 57).

The process of studying politics must, consequently be attuned to this reality, which is why it is necessary to devise a method that acknowledges and takes into consideration the many interrelated levels of politics. To be able to study the political, it is imperative that we follow an approach akin to what has been called 'the sociological imagination', by C. Wright Mills in a book by that title. That is, to study political participation we must have the

capacity to shift to shift from one perspective to another – from the political to the psychological; from examination of a single family to comparative assessment of the national budgets of the world; from the theological
school to the military establishment; from considerations of an oil industry to studies of contemporary poetry. It [the sociological imagination] is
the capacity to range from the most impersonal and remote transforma-
tions to the most intimate features of the human self – and to see the relations between the two. (Mills 2002, 7).

To adopt this perspective does not imply that we abandon social science
methods, such as the comparative method. Indeed, the comparative
method contributes important insights. As Edmund Burke, the philosopher observed in *A Philosophical Enquiry into the Origin of Our Ideas of
the Sublime and the Beautiful*: 'We ought to compare our subject with
things of similar nature, and even of things of contrary nature; for discoveries may be, and often are made by the contrast, which would
escape us on the single view' (Burke 1998, 54).

In the case of political participation, examples from individual
countries cannot stand alone, but must be put into perspective.
Consequently, while this book is mainly based on analyses of participatory politics in a British context, it also contrasts findings from other
similar countries in Europe, North America and Australia.

By contrasting and comparing cases we can get a sense of general tendencies and trends, but we cannot – and should not – expect to find
general laws of political participation. Instead, what we can observe are
patterns across cases.

Thus while I analyse patterns, and even introduce theories in chapters 3 and 4, the analysis of concrete phenomena in chapters 5 to 9 will
be based on a method which deliberately avoids grand theory.

This might be criticised. What is the point of political science if it cannot
even provide us with law-like formulations and recurrent patterns? The
answer to this question is that politics is too complex a phenomenon to
be subjected to a 'scientific' study. The study of politics, very much like
detective work, is an endeavour which requires us to draw on many
sources and clues, but always with the overall aim of finding a plot. To
understand political events – like why governments decide to hold referendums (see chapter 8) or what determines the level of electoral turnout
in elections (chapter 3) – we need to look for 'certain fundamental concepts, which run like red threads through the whole' (Arendt 2000, 112).

Positivist political science is often based on a rather crude imitation
of the natural sciences. The phenomenological study of the subject
(which concentrates on finding the 'plot'), on the other hand, has a more
illustrious philosophical pedigree, going all the way back to Aristotle.

In his *Poetics*, Aristotle saw it as the aim of literature to uncover the plot. The same is true for political science:

> In writing his Odyssey he [Homer] did not put everything that happened to Odysseus . . . for it was not a matter of necessity . . . that either of these incidents should have led to other: on the contrary, he constructed the Odyssey round a single action (Aristotle 1965, 43).

That is, in analysing the concrete case we seek to understand the plot or logic that applies to this case, but not necessarily to other cases. We analyse political phenomena like we analyse a novel or a play! Hence, doing political science 'is like trying to read (in the sense of "construct a reading of") a manuscript – foreign, faded, full of ellipses, incoherencies, suspicious emendations, and tendentious commentaries, but written not in conventional graphs of sounds but in transient examples of shaped behaviour' (Geertz 1973, 10).

In analysing political participation, we must (as I try to do in the final three chapters) use a *verstehen* (understanding) approach. This is one of the reasons why political science is a complicated subject to study, for, to invoke Hans-Georg Gadamer, political participation, being a cultural phenomenon, is often concerned with experiences that 'lie outside science', and is consequently concerned with experiences which 'cannot be verified by the methodological means proper to science' (Gadamer 2004, xxi).

While political science in Britain has traditionally been based on a 'narratological approach', this has rarely been made subject to detailed analysis (Page 1990; Qvortrup 2004). As British (and Australian) political scientists are being constantly challenged by positivist approaches (especially from North America), it is worth sketching an outline of a justification for adopting this approach.

Individuals do not readily engage in politics, and the politics of participation deals with those extraordinary situations when the 'people' – for a variety of reasons – do become engaged in political activities. Hence political participation is about more than reason and rationality: it is also about passion and engagement. To be sure, there may be certain things that often trigger mass protests, but the exact nature of political action is always an unknown. It is because of this that political deeds – by their very nature – can never be understood in terms of an overarching theory. This brings us back to contemporary political science, the problem with which is that it is based on what we might call *the hypothesis of conformism*, i.e. the view that individuals conform to the already established patterns. This view is especially pertinent in economics and statistics – the disciplines on which much recent political science – e.g. rational-choice theory – is based (Shepsle and Bonchek 1997).

Friedrich Nietzsche once observed – perhaps slightly tongue in cheek:

Statistics proves that there are laws in history. Yes, it proves how vulgar and disgustingly uniform the masses are. You should have kept statistics in Athens. Then you would have sensed the difference. The more inferior and unindividual the masses are, the more rigorous the statistical laws. (1995, 208)

Modern political science seems to positively endorse this 'disgusting' uniformity by insisting on looking for recurrent patterns even among events that are plainly unique, such as the East Germans' demonstrations in front of the Berlin Wall in 1989. The result of this is that 'everything distinct disappears and everything that is new and shocking is (not explained but) explained away either through drawing some analogies or reducing it to a previously known chain of causes and influences' (Arendt 2000, 163).

This approach is fundamentally at odds with the models of political science developed by humanist thinkers like Aristotle and Machiavelli and their modern followers. To recapture those elements of political practice, Hannah Arendt has suggested that the Machiavellian concept of *virtū* provides a possible escape route. *Virtū*, according to Arendt, is

best rendered by 'virtuosity', that is, an excellence we attribute to the performing arts . . . where accomplishment lies in the performance itself . . .[The] virtuosoship of . . . *virtū* somehow reminds us of the fact . . . that the Greeks always used such metaphors as flute playing, dancing, healing, and seafaring to distinguish political from other activities, that is, they drew their analogies from those arts in which virtuosity of performance is decisive. (1983, 153)

In other words, 'since all acting contains an element of virtuosity, and because virtuosity is an excellence we ascribe to the performing arts, politics has often been defined as an art' (ibid., 153). Applied to individuals who engage in political participation, we can argue that they, rather like the Homeric *hērōs*, create stories out of their lives by contributing to the shaping of the societies in which they live. Some might find this claim far-fetched and a little over the top. It is not! The Greek *hērō* was not unique: his action was 'no other than [that of which] every free man was capable' (Arendt quoted in Kristeva 2001, 72).

Politics is not rocket science. It is much more difficult! We can, therefore, hope to understand it only if we are willing to study all aspects of political participation with an open mind, in the hope of uncovering an underlying plot in a concrete case. The best way of doing this is not by developing esoteric mathematical formulae (though they do have a place in the overall system), but by engaging with the political reality.

Richard Fenno has described this approach as 'soaking and poking'. His explanation provides a fitting epitaph to this introductory section:

> Someone doing this kind of research is quite likely to have no crystallised idea of what he or she is looking for or what questions to ask when he or she starts. Researchers typically become interested in some observable set of activities and decide to go and have a firsthand look at them. They fully expect that an open-minded exposure to events in the milieu and to the perspectives of those with whom they interact will produce ideas that might never have occurred to them otherwise. Only after prolonged soaking is the problem formulated. (1990, 57)

2

Participation and democracy from the Greeks to our times

Theoretical and historical aspects of citizen politics

Whatever its form, citizen politics is based on the premiss that citizens can play an effective and efficient role in the political process. This is far from a trivial view. It is worth remembering that citizen involvement is historically the exception (Finer 1998): for much of human history, the ordinary people have not been citizens in the modern sense of the word, but were rather subjects of more or less despotic leaders and rulers. While this book is concerned mainly with positive – as opposed to normative – issues (with *is* rather than with *ought*), it is important to stress that philosophers and political thinkers have been divided as to the merits of letting the people involve themselves in the political process. To understand the empirical questions regarding the politics of participation we need to understand also the theoretical and philosophical questions pertaining to citizen engagement in the process of governing – what Macpherson (1984) has called 'the life and times of liberal democracy'.

In a now famous article, Francis Fukuyama (1989), a State Department employee with a Ph.D in political theory, concluded that we had reached 'the end of history', as there was no legitimate alternative to liberal democracy. While his evaluation seemed to have been repudiated in the subsequent 'clash of civilisations' (Huntingdon 1996), the thrust of Fukuyama's argument still contains an element of truth.

To be sure, the argument was put rather crudely – and perhaps deliberately so. The theory, however, was not originally developed by Fukuyama, but – as he was the first to admit – by the German philosopher G.W.F. Hegel (1770–1832) and more recently by the French philosopher Alexandre Kojève (1968), who was inspired by Hegel. According to Hegel and Kojève the history of human societies was ultimately the history of freedom – and, hence, of democracy. In his *Introduction to the Philosophy of History*, Hegel argued that the whole process of historical development could be described as the unfolding of freedom: in the ancient empires of Egypt, Assyria and China, only one individual was free – the supreme ruler; later, e.g. in the Middle Ages, some (men) were free; and finally in the modern age all adults have been free (Hegel 1988, 93–106). Needless to say, the process of liberation and democratisation was never in fact that smooth.

Hegel – and Kojève with him – emphasised that the growth of freedom had come about as a result of a long process of what he called *dialectic*, a kind of historical 'ping-pong' between different ideas, which gradually resulted in the triumph of liberty. That is, the advances in freedom were often counted by set-backs (e.g. when the caesars – or the emperors – in Rome abolished the republic). In Hegel's optic, the development of freedom could be likened to a great debate between historical epochs, in which ideas of freedom were finally prevailing (Hegel 1988, 22). Plainly, not even Hegel believed that things had progressed so neatly (Kojève 1968, 15), but his grand theory – even if we do not agree with it – provides us with a point of reference with which we can compare more recent theories.

Moreover, at a time when support for democracy is an unquestioned article of faith it is worth asking if this system of government is really as secure as we tend to believe. Any serious thinking about citizen politics must consider whether freedom has come about as some kind of natural law or whether it is a right that must be earned afresh by each generation – as Goethe suggested in Faust, 'only he deserves freedom like life who must conquer it anew each day' (Goethe 1958, 331; my translation).

Athens and democracy

It is difficult to write about democracy in the ancient world: we have few sources and accounts, and those we have were written by participant observers like Plato and Cicero who were openly partial, and never *wertfrei* and neutral observers. Any assessment of ancient Greece and Rome must, therefore, be read in this light.

It was the Greeks in the Athenian city–state (or *polis*) who first developed something resembling what we understand to be citizen politics. In the fourth century BC, the Athenians practised a system of direct democracy which allowed all adult, property-owning, male citizens to participate directly in making the laws of the republic. The central institution in ancient Athens was the Assembly of the People (*ecclesia*) in which *all* citizens (as long as they were male property owners!) participated, irrespective of income, with the right to choose *archons* 'by allotment from a short list of men elected by each of the tribes' (Aristotle 1984, 49).

The Greeks – like the Australians and Belgians a couple of millennia later – took civic responsibilities very seriously. In present-day Australia and Belgium, voters are fined for not voting in general elections, and in Greece it was the same; as Aristotle observed, 'if a member of the council was absent from a meeting . . . he would be fined three drachmae' (ibid., 45).

Paradoxically, we know of the normative justification of Athenian democracy mainly from its two staunchest critics, namely Plato and the historian Thucydides – though we have also the fragmentary comments of other writers, for example, the playwright Euripides (Euripides 1958). Plato, however, is the main source, and for all his seeming elitism in *The Republic* and *The Laws*, his *Protagoras* (admittedly an early dialogue) presents one of the most compelling justifications of democracy. While Plato the aristocrat was at best lukewarm in his disposition towards the 'rule of the people', he let Protagoras tell a tale which is worth quoting at length:

> Zeus was afraid that our whole race might be wiped out, so he sent Hermes to bring justice and a sense of shame to humans, so that there would be order within cities and bonds of friendship to unite them . . . Hermes asked Zeus how he should distribute shame and justice to humans, should I distribute them as the other arts were? This is how the others were distributed: one person practising the art of medicine suffices for many ordinary people; and so forth with the other practitioners. Should I establish justice and shame among humans in this way, or distribute it to all? 'To all', said Zeus, 'and let all have a share. For cities would never come to be if only a few possessed these, as is the case with the other arts . . . And so it is . . . that when the Athenians (and others as well) are debating architectural excellence, or the virtue proper to any other professional [specialism], they think that only a few individuals have the right to advise them, and they do not accept advice from anyone outside these . . . but when the debate involved political excellence, which must proceed entirely from justice and temperance, they accept advice from anyone, and with good reason, for they think that this particular civic or political virtue is shared by all, or there would not be any cities. (Plato 1997, *Protagoras*, 322c–323a)

Plato was not the only opponent of democracy to have provided a seemingly fair-minded platform for his opponents. Thucydides, an Athenian general who had grown increasingly unhappy about the democratic republic's lack of decisiveness in the Peloponnesian War against Sparta (a famously non-democratic state), nevertheless recorded Pericles's funeral oration – which over time has become one of the classic justifications of democracy. Our system of government,

observed Pericles 'favours the many instead of the few; this is why its
called a democracy' (Thucydides 1951, 104). That he equated democracy with the rule of the many did not imply, however, that he merely
favoured a system of majority rule. Like modern radical democrats, he
championed deliberation and emphasised the idea of democracy by discussion:

> Instead of looking at discussion as a stumbling-block in the way of action,
> we think it an indispensable preliminary to any wise action at all . . . in
> our enterprises we present a singular spectacle of daring and deliberation.
> (Pericles in Thucydides 1951, 105)

As it will be observed, these cases democracy were based on high prin-
ciples, which were (at least in the case of Protagoras) based on theological justifications.

Such arguments are unlikely to convince us today – and nor did they
persuade all intellectuals, politicians and even citizens in former times.
Aristotle, Plato's pupil and the father of empirical political science, was
keen to base his observations and his recommendations on facts rather
than on lofty speculations. To do so, he developed a taxonomy of different political regime types, depending on the number of rulers, and
sought – on the basis of this – to arrive at conclusions either for or
against citizen politics.

Inspired by a distinction outlined by Plato in *The Republic* (1997,
544a), Aristotle, distinguished between six types of government (1988,
1279a 25ff.): monarchy, aristocracy and constitutionalism were ideal
instances of government by, respectively, one individual, a few individuals or many citizens; but for each of these three ideals Aristotle
found counter-cases of degenerate rule. Thus monarchy could easily
develop into tyranny, aristocracy into oligarchy and constitutionalism
into mob-rule.

This taxonomy of regime forms served more than a descriptive
purpose. The aim of Aristotle's politics is 'to consider what form of political community is best for those who are most able to realise their
idea of life' (ibid., 1260b 27). Aristotle did not – and was unwilling – to

Table 2.1 Aristotle's forms of government

Ideal form	*Degenerate form*
Monarchy	Tyranny
Aristocracy	Oligarchy
Constitutionalism	Democracy

Source: Aristotle, *The Politics.*

conclude with mathematical precision which system of government was best (2004, 1094b 15). On the basis of extensive empirical observations, he concluded that in certain circumstances monarchy was the preferable form, e.g. when

> a whole family, or some individual, happens to be so pre-eminent in excellence as to surpass all others, then it is just that they should be the royal family and supreme over all, or that this one citizen should be King. (Ibid., 1288a 15)

However, Aristotle, empiricist as he was, acknowledged that the rule of monarchs could degenerate and that 'the greatest crimes are caused by excess and not by necessity' (ibid., 1267a 14). Further, he readily acknowledged that the many are more incorruptible than the 'few' (1286a 31). In practice, therefore, Aristotle preferred the rule of the many, i.e. a constitutional democracy:

> The view that the multitude, rather than a few good men, should be sovereign . . . would perhaps be true. For although each member of the multitude is not a good man, still it is possible that when they come together, they should be better – not as individuals but collectively, just as a feast to which many contribute is better than a dinner provided out of a single purse. For each individual has a share of excellence and practical wisdom, and when they meet together, just as they become in a manner one man, who has many feet, and hands, and senses, so too with regard to their character and thought. Hence the many are better judges than a single man of music and poetry, for some understand one part, and some another, and among them they understand the whole. (Ibid., 1281a 40–1281b 9)

Given this conclusion, allied to observations like 'the basis of democracy is liberty' (1317 40), it is tempting to elevate Aristotle to the Parthenon of democratic champions. While in many ways he was a remarkably modern thinker, we must not forget that he held a fair number of opinions that are unpalatable to us. He held women in low regard (he approvingly cited Sophocles's infamous dictum 'Silence is a woman's glory' (1260a 30) and argued avidly for slavery (1255b 29). Not all the conclusions of the classical writers have stood the test of time.

But Aristotle did not provide only a theoretical case for democracy. As the father of political science – and a dozen other sciences as well – he was also an empirical commentator who described actual institutions. According to Aristotle's *Athenian Constitution*, the central institution in ancient Athens was the Assembly of the People. This body debated the policies proposed by the 'Council of the 500', a body chosen by lot, from whose number 9 *archons* (literally, 'rulers') were chosen to run daily affairs. In a modern simplification, it could be said that the 'Council of the 500' performed the functions of a 'parliament', while the archons formed a group not dissimilar to that of the 'cabinet' in a modern state.

Initially membership of the Council was restricted to the richest citizens. This bias towards the rich was, however, removed in the 450s when all male citizens over the age of 30 became eligible to this body (Möckli 1994, 43) and acquired the right to select by lot the *archons* (Finley 1983, 73).

Yet, as is often the case when dealing with politics, our knowledge is incomplete; we must rely on all manner of evidence to patch together a coherent picture. Solon (according to legend, the founder of the Athenian system of government) boasted that he 'stood covering both [the rich and the poor] with a strong shield, permitting neither to triumph unjustly over the other' (Solon quoted in ibid., 1). Whether we should believe him is another matter: Solon was, after all, a politician. Yet the claimed balance between the classes was also cited in popular culture at the time. Thus in Euripides's *Suppliant Women*, one character observes: 'This city is ruled by no one man. The *demos* reigns, taking turns annually [. . .] They do not give supremacy to the rich; the poor man has an equal share in it' (Euripides 1958, 399 and 419). Of course, Euripides may have had an axe to grind, but the fact that democracy was sufficiently embedded to be alluded to in a popular play says something about its centrality to Athenian society – and about the people's involvement in the system.

But Athenian democracy, for all its strengths, was not a panacea. Archaeologists have found evidence of fraudulent voting in cases where the Assembly was to vote on expulsion from the city (known as *ostracism*). Recently pre-prepared ballots, dated to circa 200 BC have been found, 'all [bearing] the name of Themistocles, written in small hand, clearly prepared beforehand for distribution among potential voters but in the end not used' (Finley 1983, 50). In addition to evidence of fraud, there are indications of low turnout by the citizenry: historians of ancient Greece have estimated that only 6,000 of the 40,000 citizens regularly took part in the proceedings on the – typically – 40 occasions when the *ecclesia* met each year (Hansen 1976, 115). On the other hand, the fact that 'in any decade, something between a fourth and a third of the total citizenry would have been council members', i.e. *archons* (Finley 1983, 74), suggests that the level of citizen participation in Athens was considerably higher than in any currently known democracy. Moreover, the system of government in Athens was freer than that in which today's politics operates. In the twenty-first century, politics is dominated by political parties – mechanisms of direct democracy notwithstanding. In Athens circa 450 BC it was all rather different: the 'debates were "real": there were no formal party line-ups, no whips, no machinery to predetermine the final vote irrespective of the speech-making. It was . . . in debates that leadership was tested, that politics were made and unmade" (Finley 1983, 76)

The Romans and the Middle Ages

Like the Athenians, the Romans (until mid-first century BC) practised a democracy of sorts. The Romans called their system of government a 'republic' (the word comes from the Latin *res publica*, which literally means 'public things'). In our day 'republic' signifies that a system of government is ultimately based on the will of the people. As the original meaning of the words indicates, this did not always apply to the Roman system of government, which existed from circa 300 BC to 49 BC. The Roman republic was – at least formally – based on popular consent, but its system of government was arguably more elitist than that of Athens during the days of Pericles.

The contribution of the Romans to democratic thinking is often overlooked in political science (Millar 2002). The cradle of democracy – we are often told – stood in Athens. Yet, Roman ideas of government have in many ways been almost as influential in the history of political thought, not least because the Romans practised a form of representative government – with many elements of direct democracy thrown in. In the eighteenth century, James Madison, one of the founders of the American Constitution, frequently cited examples from Rome to support his views, as also did Rousseau and, in particular, Niccoló Machiavelli whose main contribution to democratic thinking, the *Discorsi*, was a commentary on the Roman historian Titus Livius's history of the republic. No summary of the history of democracy would be complete without mention of the Romans.

There is considerable disagreement among historians as to whether the Roman republic is correctly described as 'democratic' (e.g. Jehne 1995), and some have taken a rather harsh view of the republic. M.I. Finley, a classical historian, has stressed that 'the narrowness of the activities allowed to the assemblies [of the people] cannot be overstressed, at least with respect to the citizenry at large' (1983, 91). While the debate continues, there is a tendency among today's scholars to take a more charitable view. Recently Fergus Millar (2002, 6–7) has argued that, 'far from being a tightly controlled, "top–down" system, the late Republic was on the contrary a very striking example of a political system in which rival conceptions of state and society . . . were openly debated before the crowd in the Forum'. While others offer a less charitable interpretation (e.g. Finley 1983, 87), it is fair to say that 'voting was a major occupation of the citizen who lived in Republican Rome or were there when the assemblies met' (Taylor 1966, 1).

Rome was never as democratic as Athens, where there were few distinctions between the citizens. Rome's citizens, by contrast, were divided into *patricians* and *plebeians*. In the Roman republic the consuls (or chief magistrates) were elected by popular vote by the *comitia centuriata* (which included both patricians and plebeians). In Athens, as we have seen, the *archons* were chosen by lot and the highest positions were open to all citizens – and we have evidence to suggest that the Council of the 500 represented a broad cross-section of society. In Rome, by contrast, the highest posts were *de facto* reserved for the *patricius*. To be sure, 'public office could be gained only by direct election in which all (adult) male citizens, including free slaves, had the right to vote and all legislation was subject to direct popular voting' (Millar 2002, 11). It has often been argued that the richest exercised an undue influence over the other citizens and were seemingly able to 'buy votes' to secure the result (Finley 1983, 91). There are, no doubt examples of this, yet the fact that the Romans – unlike the Athenians – cast their ballots in secret indicates that there were limits to the patricians' attempts to rig the vote.

Whereas Athenian democracy was based on a relatively simple divide between the citizens and ruling council, Roman government was based on an intricate system of checks and balances between several assemblies, councils and elected officers (Cicero 1998, 157). 'Structurally, or constitutionally if one prefers, there were fundamental differences at every point. [In Rome] there were not one assembly but four' (Finley 1983, 83). These were, respectively, the *comitia centuriata*, the *comitia curiata* (an electoral college), the *comitia tribute* – the latter performing the major role of legislative organ (Millar 2002, 7); in addition the Council of the People (*concilium plebis*), which represented only the the poor, could enact legislation by so-called *plebi scita*.

I should not fail to mention that this system was tempered by the Senate. This body considered mainly of former executives (e.g. consuls) who *de facto* served for life (Finley 1983, 88). The Senate had considerable powers, and it was, in Finlay's view, 'hardly ever possible to take any governmental action in Rome unless and until the Senate approved' (ibid.). The power of this 'super-elite body of life members' was evident not only in legislation but in the everyday administration (*auctoritas*) of politics. Thus in cases of 'a threat to the safety of the state' (ibid., 4), the senators could declare a state of emergency – a *senatus consultum ultimum*, i.e. a proclamation of a so-called *iustitium*, meaning 'standstill' or 'suspension of the law' (Cicero 1998, 157). The result was that 'the "subversive" elements were . . . treated as enemies of the state, outlaws (and were sometimes formally declared as such), [and] no longer entitled to the protection of the law, in particular the right to a fair trial' (Finley 1983, 3).

The Senate was the 'keystone' of the Roman system of government, and according to Finley this 'body may properly be called a government' (ibid., 88). Although a most important body, however, the Senate was not a legislature – 'that role belonged to the *populus Romanus* itself, or rather to those citizens who were present in the Forum when the moment came for them to form themselves into the thirty-five voting units, or *tribus*, that constituted the normal form of legislative assembly, the *comitia tribute*' (Millar 2002, 7). Moreover, we have evidence from the contemporary Roman historian Sallust to suggest that the decisions reached by the Senate could be – and occasionally were – invalidated by the tribunes (ibid., 52). While elitist, the Roman republic did have elements of democracy – though not in the pure form known from Greece.

This system began to change towards the end of the republic. In 88 BC Sulla, then the Consul, passed a series of directives which stripped the Council of the People of its legislative functions, which were transferred to the *comitia centuriata*. This body, which had previously served the function of an kind of electoral college (it chose the consuls), was now given legislative power. While these reforms were overturned after Sulla's death, the influence of the plebeians arguably continued to decline until the introduction of dictatorship by Gaius Julius Caesar and his successors who concentrated more and more power in their own hands, e.g. by having themselves elected to various magistracies for life.

The death of the Roman republic finally came when Caesar Augustus transferred the legislative functions of the popular assemblies to the Senate and the senators, who were appointed by the Emperor. The ancient world's experiment with democracy had ended at the time when Rome was at its zenith.

The Romans have never enjoyed the same democratic reputation as the Athenians, although both, through Cicero, left an important legacy in political thought. However, they were doers more than thinkers like their Mediterranean neighbours. To be sure, Cicero (106–43 BC) and Seneca (4 BC–65 AD) wrote insightful essays about the rule of the people; yet, for all their merits, those writings contributed little of substance to the debate. At the risk of oversimplifying, a case could be made for the view that the democratic – though not the political! – debate stagnated from the time of Aristotle until the thirteenth century.

While the so-called 'Dark Ages' were short on democratic debate, it is important to have at least an idea of the political thinking which shaped that period. Christian thinkers by and large did not write much about democracy – let alone about government. This is, perhaps, not surprising. Jesus himself reportedly had been less than enthusiastic about politics, having claimed 'My kingdom is not of this world' (John 18.36) and, according to the earlier gospel of Matthew (22.21), having unequivocally declared that people should 'Render . . . unto Caesar the things which are Caesar's and unto God the things that are God's' – not a view that seems to chime with running a world empire!

St Augustine, the foremost writer on government in the early centuries of Christianity, consequently took the view that Christians generally should wait for the Second Coming and, in the meantime, accept that all rulers – even the most despotic – were there by the grace of God (Augustine 1984, 176). Christians should not attempt to establish a democracy, but should serve the powers that be, as even the most despotic rule would be preferable to anarchy. Augustine, in other words, did not hold out hope for any immediate solutions to political problems. As he puts it in *De civitate Dei* (*The City of God*): 'True justice . . . does not exist other than in the commonwealth whose founder and ruler is Christ' (1984, 73). That is, a politician should not deceive himself into thinking that she or he can create a perfect world. A statesman could, at best, hope to perform good stewardship until God decided – to establish the *ecclesia praedestinata* – the perfect commonwealth for those predestined to live in his presence.

Augustine was not, however, indifferent to the form of government that should exist until the return of Christ. Indeed, Augustine would have preferred a Christian emperor – an *imperator Christianus* – a virtuous man inspired by God, who was willing to perform the selfless duties of a servant to the people (ibid., 213). But he had no illusions about the prospects of even the most pious of rulers. As he said, *remota justitia quid sunt regna nisi latrocinia magna* – 'even those states that adopt justice are nothing but bands of thieves' (ibid., 177).

Like Augustine, the political thinkers of the Middle Ages were inclined towards monarchy – indeed no less a person than Dante Alighieri (1265–1321) wrote a treatise (*De Monarchia*) in defence of this system of government, in which he argued that the powers of the monarch were derived from God, and that only the rule of a universal king could resolve political problems (Dante 1979).

But things began gradually to change after the (re)appraisal of Aristotle's writings in the twelfth and thirteenth centuries, when (after contact with the more advanced Arabic culture) writers became aware of his thinking, which had been all but forgotten in the meantime. Unable to follow the Macedon master's taste for a form of democracy, the Italian philosopher and theologian Thomas Aquinas (1224–1274) considered in *De regimine principum* that the people should have a right to rebel against kings whose rule were inconsistent with natural law (Aquinas 2002, 18). Admittedly, upholding the right to rebel did not make Aquinas into anything like a democrat, let alone a defender of the rule of the people. But by granting the people a political right, he arguably paved the way for Marsilius of Padua (1275–1342) who, in *Defensor pacis* (*The Defender of Peace*, written in 1324), proposed that all sovereignty rests with the people: 'The whole body of citizens or its majority alone is the human legislator' (Marsilius 2005, 309).

As so often has been the case in the history of democratic thinking, these ideas emerged in response to particular political developments, namely Pope John XXII's refusal to accept Louis of Bavaria's rule as emperor. Marsilius – we must assume – did not set out to become a democratic theorist. But to counter the Pope's argument he needed to establish an alternative theory, namely that power *ultimately* rested with the people (McClelland 1996, 142). He was motivated by the conviction that 'decrees of the bishop of Rome, or of any other bishops or body of bishops, have no power to coerce anyone by secular penalties or punishments, except by the authorization of the human legislator' (Marsilius 2005, 311), i.e. the people. Having reached this conclusion, he needed an alternative to the ideology of papal supremacy, and found it in the belief that the

> *legislator* alone or the one who rules by its authority has the power to dispense with human laws. The elective principality or other office derives its authority from the election of the body having the right to elect, and not from the confirmation or approval of any other power. (Ibid., 311)

Often mentioned in the political theories of citizen politics, Marsilius's insistence on the right of the people to govern proved a turning point in political thinking. But as is often the case, it is difficult to say whether Marsilius was a product of his time or whether the subsequent debates were a result of his genius. Certainly his writings are insightful, though they are occasionally quoted out of context by present-day commentators.

But why was democracy suddenly back in vogue? What accounted for this new interest in democratic thinking? One answer favoured by historians is that the economic independence of a growing number of northern Italy's small city–states (Roberts 1980, 480) had recreated (after an interval of a millennium) the conditions for a political system along the same lines as ancient Athens' and the early Roman republic's. These new economic conditions made the monarchical ideas of the Middle Ages appear obsolete to the independently minded proto-capitalists of Padua, Genoa and Florence, and gave rise to an impressive array of thinkers who, through their questioning of the foundations of the monarchical government, paved the way for democracy.

Machiavelli and the Renaissance

It is perhaps in the nature of things that rapid and momentous change gives rise to that philosophical bewilderment which is necessary to the generation of grand ideas and new departures. One thinker who contributed to a quantum leap in democratic thinking – his subsequent reputation notwithstanding – was the Florentine political theorist Niccolò Machiavelli.

A writer most famous for his cynical treatise *Il principe*, (*The Prince*) which has been read as a defence of tyranny, Machiavelli was, in many ways, the first theoretician since Aristotle to assess the merits of despotism against those of democracy. Assuming that 'he who diligently examines past events easily foresees the future [and] can apply to them remedies used by the ancients' (Machiavelli 1965, 278), he sought to understand the rationale behind and the consequences of the citizens' right to govern their own affairs.

It was Machiavelli's great insight that a great state must remain free of both internal servitude and externally imposed oppression (ibid., 195). A free state will – or is most likely to – grow if 'the people are in control' of their lives (ibid., 316). In stating his preference for republican – or democratic – government over tyranny, Machiavelli made it clear that under a dictatorship – or monarchical government – 'what benefits him [the ruler] usually injures the city'. Consequently, he concluded that 'all cities and provinces that live in freedom anywhere in the World always make great gains' (ibid., 332).

Machiavelli provided what we might call a utilitarian case for citizens politics: give the people a say in their own affairs and the result will be improved conditions for the many rather than for the few. This, incidentally, was a view to which thinkers returned again and again in the following centuries, and is notable especially in Madison's and Schumpeter's arguments for (representative) democracy.

For all their insights and skill, however, it was not the radical Italian thinkers like Machiavelli and Marsilius who paved the way for modern democracy in its current form. Indeed, while democracy staged something of a comeback in the Renaissance, it was by no means plain sailing for popular government from the sixteenth century onwards. In fact, the debate about the pros and cons of democracy positively resembled the

Hegelian dialectical process from the time of Machiavelli until the middle of the twentieth century: from the opposition of two contradictory ideas – democracy and its antithesis – new and more adequate notions emerged. Machiavelli's ideas were immediately opposed by Jean Bodin and King James I, both of whom maintained that sovereignty was instituted by God and that monarchical government was therefore to be preferred. (These ideas, in true Hegelian fashion, were, in due course, countered by the democratic ideas of the Levellers, as will be seen.)

In England, this new idea of divinely sanctioned monarchy was strongly promoted by James I (1566–1625) who, in *The Trew Law of Free Monarchies* (1598), defended the monarchy as a God-given institution and warned against the 'siren songs' of those who praised or excused rebellions. However, James's position did not prove popular at the time. In constant battle with the House of Commons about his demands for tax-increases, he created the conditions for the English Civil War, which culminated in the execution of his son and successor, Charles I, and the establishment of a republican system of government under the leadership of Oliver Cromwell.

The Civil War gave rise to an abundance of political tracts – democratic and otherwise. Thomas Hobbes's *Leviathan* (1651) is justly famous for its non-theological case for absolutism and for the insistence that the only bulwark against social disintegration and war is the establishment of a strong central government.

Less well known in the history of ideas are the men who developed the arguments for democracy. Cromwell himself was positively inclined towards representative government, but for all his egalitarianism was unwilling, unlike the Levellers, to extend the franchise to all. The Levellers were men from Cromwell's New Model Army who advocated all but universal suffrage in a series of drafts of a basic democratic constitution, known as *An Agreement of the Free People of England* (Hampsher-Monk 1976). In addition to advocating a very modern conception of representative democracy, the Levellers held that the people should have the power to recall representatives – an idea which was also important to US populists of the late twentieth and the early twenty-first century, when it was used by, for example, Arnold Schwarzenegger to recall Governor Grey Davis and win the Californian governorship for himself in 2003.

These ideas were far out in the future for the Levellers, whose influence declined and disappeared when monarchy was re-instituted in the 1660s. While ultimately unsuccessful, the Levellers had taken the arguments about democracy to a new level, even though the pendulum swung back to the defence of theocratic absolutism as proposed by Robert Filmer (1949) in his treatise *Patriarcha, or the Natural Power of Kings* (1680).

Democracy comes of age: representative democracy

Today, most people take it for granted that politics and democracy revolves around representative institutions such as the Houses of Parliament and the US Congress. It is, however, only relatively recently that democracy and representative institutions have been equated, an identification that was hailed as a triumph for the science of politics. It was, in the words of James Mill (father of John Stuart Mill) 'the grand discovery of modern times' in which 'the solution of all difficulties, both speculative and practical, would be found' (quoted in Held 1996, 119).

For the ancients, and indeed, the thinkers up until the French Revolution, democracy meant direct democracy, i.e. government by the citizens themselves. This did not mean that the writers were unfamiliar with representative institutions; they just called them something else.

For Rousseau – who endorsed a system of representatives kept in check by the people through referendums – the term 'the elected aristocracy' meant what we today understand as representative democracy.

However, the general acceptance of representative government as a necessary and desirable institution of democracy was still one century away. Even Locke, the father of liberalism, observed that 'if a controversy arises between the Prince and some of the people . . . I think the proper *Umpire* in such a case should be the body of the *people*' (Locke 1988, 427). But, in truth, he had little else to say about democracy and representation in his *Two Treatises of Government*. What made Locke important was not so much his theorising in the Second Treatise – though his case for property rights was to have a revolutionary effect, as it was his rejection of the theocratic ideals of and justification for monarchy that were espoused by Sir Robert Filmer in Britain (namely, the idea that politics could be based on purely theological foundations). But, whereas Filmer had argued that monarchy was the natural form of government as God had endowed Adam with the right to rule, Locke rejected this reasoning on scriptural as well as on political grounds, noting that 'all this ado about *Adam's Fatherhood*, the greatness of its power, and the necessity of its supposal, helps nothing to establish the power of those that govern' (ibid., 232).

Montesquieu, the other great author of checks and balances, likewise wrote precious little about popular government. In practical politics, it was only when the Constitutional Convention in Philadelphia in 1787 established a bi-cameral congress in a federal American republic, that representative government in anything like the modern form took root. This does not, however, imply that the Americans invented the system of representative government; nor would they themselves have claimed this. James Madison – the chief theoretician of the American Constitution – based his considerations in the *Federalist Papers* (a series of articles published by Madison, Alexander Hamilton and John Jay before the New York Assembly voted on the proposed Constitution) on the ancient republics and – more importantly to thinkers from the 'old world' – Charles Secondat du Montesquieu.

In *The Spirit of the Laws* (published in 1748), Montesquieu had argued that the greatest danger to liberty was the concentration of power in the hands of one individual or a group of individuals:

> When legislative power is united with the executive power in a single person or in a body of the magistracy, there is no liberty, because one can fear that the same monarch or senate that makes tyrannical laws will execute them tyrannically. (Montesquieu 1989, 157)

What makes Madison so important in the history of democratic theory is that he developed and elaborated on Montesquieu's model and combined it with the ideal of representative government. In *Federalist Paper* 51, he famously made a case for a system of checks and balances, noting that if 'angels were to govern men, neither external nor internal control over government would be necessary' (Hamilton, Madison and Jay 1996, 63). Madison's main argument for democracy was utilitarian: it would ensure that men were protected against each other, and the best check on men's ambitions would be other men – 'a dependence on the people is, no doubt, the primary control on the government' (ibid.).

This utilitarian principle – as we have seen – could also be discerned in Machiavelli, yet Madison's discovery was path breaking because he sought to combine his enthusiasm for the rule of the people (but not *by* the people) with a mechanism for protecting the minority from the crushing power of the majority. Madison's ideal of government was based on the idea of 'protective democracy' (Macpherson 1984); i.e. democracy is not a system which should be defended per se, but because it provides a mechanism through which rational, utility-maximising individuals can live together under optimal circumstances.

Madison was concerned about the problem of factions – what we today would call social groups or even parties. Madison's problem with democracy was that a majority, through seemingly democratic means, could 'sacrifice to its ruling passions or interests both the public good and the rights of other citizens'. To solve the problem of the tyranny of the majority, Madison proposed a particular set of constitutional arrangements, among which are the system of representative government and a large electorate. The advantage of the system of representation was that it provided a mechanism by which to

> refine and enlarge the public views, by passing them through the medium of a chosen body of citizens, whose wisdom may best discern the true interest of their country, and whose patriotism and love of justice will be least likely to sacrifice it to temporary or partial considerations. Under such a regulation, it may well happen that the public voice, pronounced by the representatives of the people, will be more consonant to the public good than if pronounced by the people themselves, convened for the purpose. (Hamilton et al. 1996, 40)

Madison was, however, aware that the system of representation could produce its own problems, one of which was that the elected representatives themselves could become an entrenched faction that would go against the public interest. To solve this problem, Madison proposed an equally novel solution: a large electorate. In Madison's view a large republic had several advantages over a small one. In the first place, as 'each representative will be chosen by a greater number of citizens in the large than in the small republic, it will be more difficult for unworthy candidates to practice with success the vicious arts by which elections are too often carried'. More importantly, a large republic would make it unlikely – from a simple mathematical point of view – that the majority could oppress a minority, for 'the greater variety of parties and interest' in a large republic makes it 'less probable that a majority . . . will have a common motive to invade the rights of other citizens; or if such a common motive exists, it will be difficult for all who feel it to discover their own strength and to act in unison with each other' (ibid., 83). In other words, the different majorities would cancel each other out, and it would be all but impossible for a majority to suppress minorities. For Madison representative democracy in a large republic would solve two problems: the tyranny of the majority and despotism. It provided a means of ensuring a protective form of democracy which, through checks and balances, would safeguard minorities. This model of protective democracy was to be the norm in many Western democracies.

By the early twentieth century, the idea of representative government had become almost synonymous with democracy. Writers like Michels (1911) – as well as the Italians Geatano Mosca and Vilfredo Pareto who wrote at the same time – had persuasively argued that all human organisations tended to become oligarchies. The idea of protective democracy found its most eloquent twentieth-century spokesman in the Austrian-born Josef A. Schumpeter who, in *Capitalism, Socialism, and Democracy* (1951, 269), defined democracy not as the rule of the people but as 'that institutional arrangement for arriving at political decisions in which individuals acquire the power to decide by means of a competitive struggle for the people's vote'). He went on to criticise the classical understanding of democracy, arguing that it did

> not mean and cannot mean that the people actually rule in any obvious sense of the terms 'people' and 'rule.' Democracy means only that the people have the opportunity of accepting or refusing the men who are to rule them. But since they might decide this also in entirely undemocratic ways, we have had to narrow our definition by adding a further criterion identifying the democratic method, viz., free competition among would-be leaders for the vote of the electorate. (Ibid.)

The empirical basis of this statement is – to put it mildly – questionable (as we shall see later in this book). What is important for now, however, is not the veracity of Schumpeter's and Madison's models, but the fact that they inaugurated a wholly new way of thinking about democracy, one based both on indirect rule and on utilitarian arguments. Their models were pragmatic institutionalist schemes based on what would ensure prosperity and the protection of negative rights.

This minimalist account of democracy has been criticised by those who believe that government is also about human flourishing and the freedom to fulfil our potential. The model of protective democracy, according to Macpherson (1984, 43), was based on utilitarian assumptions about human beings rather than on real enthusiasm for self-governance:

> It's advocacy is based on the assumption than man is an infinite consumer, that his overriding motivation is to maximize his flow of satisfaction . . . Responsible government, even to the extend of responsibility to a democratic electorate, was needed for the protection of individuals and the promotion of the Gross National Product.

It is this emphasis on the pragmatic aspects of democracy that distinguishes the model of protective democracy from the ideal of developmental democracy proposed by the English philosopher John Stuart Mill and – though in a different way – by the Swiss political thinker Jean-Jacques Rousseau.

Mill's *Considerations on Representative Government* (first published in 1861) was important in making a case for representative democracy. While Mill acknowledged that there was a 'radical distinction . . . between controlling the business of government and actually doing it' (1991, 229–230), he stressed that the key justification for democracy was that it provided a prime mechanism for moral self-development and the 'highest and harmonious' expansion of individual capacities. Mill advocated the public education 'which every citizen of Athens received from her democratic institutions', and contrasted these engaged citizens favourably to 'those who have done nothing in their lives but drive a quill, or sell goods over the counter'. The private citizen, he noted, is

> called upon, while so engaged, to weigh interests not his own; to be guided, in case of conflicting claims, by another rule than his private partialities; to apply, at every turn, principles of maxims which have for their reason of existence the common good. (Ibid., 255)

He went on to argue that from these 'considerations it is evident that the only government which [could] fully satisfy all the exigencies of a social state is one in which the whole people participates' (Mill 1991, 255–256). Yet for all his seeming enthusiasm for the edifying effects of political participation, Mill concluded – without offering any justification – that 'since all cannot, in a community exceeding a single small town, participate personally in any but some very minor portions of public business, it follows that the ideal type of perfect government must be representative' (ibid., 256). Mill, it seems, was unwilling to follow his own logic.

One of the thinkers who spurred Mill to develop these ideas was the French aristocrat and politician Alexis de Tocqueville. In 1831, Tocqueville had travelled to America to study its penitentiary system. While Tocqueville and his travel companion Gustave de Beaumont duly wrote a report of their findings, entitled *Du systeme penitentiaire aux Etats-Unis et de son application en France*, which won the French Academy's Montyon Prize, it was Tocqueville's subsequent book, *De la démocratie en Amérique* (*Democracy in America*, 1988), that secured for him a lasting place in the history of political ideas and political sociology.

Tocqueville was not an unequivocal admirer of modern democracy. He was concerned about the consequences that an egalitarian society might have on individual freedom. But he was also aware that the emergence of a pluralist society had positive political implications. One of the consequences of a democratic society was that it fostered civic-spiritness:

> When the members of a community are forced to attend to public affairs, they are necessarily drawn from the circle of their own interests, and snatched at times from self-observation. As soon as a man begins to treat of public affairs in public, he begins to perceive that he is not so independent of his fellow-men as he had at first imagined, and that, in order to obtain their support, he must often lend them his co-operation. (Ibid., 433)

To ensure this, the citizens would have to learn democracy by practising it. This would be accomplished, not through constant engagement with high politics, but by taking part in communal activities, e.g. in sporting clubs and small civic organisations, which could be 'considered as large free schools, where all the members of the community go to learn the general theory of association' (ibid., 442).

It was Tocqueville's big idea that it was these *moeurs* (mores), which ultimately created a society's stable democracy, not its institutions. This view still has many followers. Indeed, in his influential study *Bowling Alone* (2000), political scientist Robert Putnam found that democracy in the USA is in crisis at present because citizens no longer are members of the small associations which Tocqueville regarded as essential for establishing a viable democratic system of government.

Yet, Tocqueville was not an uncritical admirer of government in the US. He was aware – as were few other democratic theorists – that both equality and democracy had a downside:

> No sooner does a government attempt to go beyond its political sphere and to enter upon this new track, than it exercises, even unintentionally, an insupportable tyranny; for a government can only dictate strict rules, the opinions which it favours are rigidly enforced, and it is never easy to discriminate between its advice and its commands. (Tocqueville 1988, 455)

Tocqueville was alarmed about the future, but he was in no doubt that he lived in a epoch of growing equality and democracy. Like Hegel – but in a less abstract way – Tocqueville was a historicist who believed in historical inevitability. In the future, he claimed, 'all the members of the community [will] take a part in the government, and . . . each one of them [will have] an equal right to take a part in it (ibid., 341).

His concerns notwithstanding, Tocqueville did not advocate a return to a bygone despotism (such as existed prior to the French Revolution). But he took a dim view of the future. Equality had many dangers, it placed 'men side by side, unconnected by any common tie; despotism [on the other hand] raises barriers to keep them asunder; the former predisposes them not to consider their fellow-creatures, the latter makes general indifference a sort of public virtue' (ibid., 421).

These ideas impressed Mill and other democrats, who saw Tocqueville as something approaching a prophet of democracy. This high regard for the French theoretician has continued until the present day and he is regularly quoted by politicians, from Democrats like Bill Clinton to Republicans like Pat Buchanan (see http://www.tocqueville.org/pitney.htm; accessed 8 September 2006).

Beyond protective democracy

For all his enthusiasm for elements of direct participation, Mill was an elitist who was unwilling to trust the people – he even proposed that graduates should have two votes! Indeed, it could be argued, as Robert Dahl has done, that his ideal of representative democracy

> removed government so far from the direct reach of the demos that one could reasonably wonder, as some critics have, whether the new system was entitled to call itself by the venerable name of democracy. (Dahl 1989, 30)

The problem with Mill and other theorists of representative government is that a ruling – albeit elected – elite, once established, threatens to replicate itself in similarly powerful, self-serving, groups. The main problem with this system is that it enables those with superior resources – above all money – to unduly influence the debate and its outcome.

As has been argued by French political scientist Maurice Duverger in *Modern Democracies* (1980, 11), the modern state is a 'pluto-democracy' because its power lies at the same time in both its people (*demos*) and its wealth (*plutos*), the latter having a disproportional influence on the outcomes of the political process. To be sure, Madison (and Mill) had been aware of this danger and had advocated the introduction of second chambers to control the elites (see Hamilton et al. 1996, 63). However, the problem with this model was that it merely enabled one elite to check another elite. Further, the problem with both Madison's and Mill's schemes was that they failed to appreciate the importance of political parties, which became the natural vehicle through which political battles were fought after 1870 or thereabouts. This, according to Robert Dahl (1989, 30), changed the picture:

> Where in the older view factionalism and conflict were believed to be destructive, political conflict came to be regarded as a normal, inevitable, even desirable part of a democratic order. Consequently the ancient belief that citizens both could and should pursue the public good rather than their private ends became more difficult to sustain, and even impossible, as 'the public good' fragmented into individual and group interests.

In addition, in order to prevent the formation of an entrenched class of self-serving elites, representative democracy also needs to create an array of egalitarian institutions to ensure, to a justifiable extent, an equal start for all, equality of opportunity for all and a high degree of social mobility.

Furthermore, representative democracy was often felt to detach and alienate 'ordinary' people who feel that they are unable to influence public policy. It was largely in response to these elitist tendencies that the American populists – inspired by Rousseau and other radicals – introduced an alternative check to the senates and second chambers proposed by Mill and Madison. The populists rejected the (Schumpeterian) idea of 'democracy'. Their critique was not unlike the one proposed by Robert Dahl (1989, 30):

> The idea of monistic democracy, in which autonomous political associations were thought to be unnecessary and illegitimate, was transformed into a pluralist political system in which autonomous associations were held to be not only legitimate but actually necessary to democracy on a large scale.

In *The Origin of Inequality*, written in 1755, Jean-Jacques Rousseau had made a case for a system of democracy in which the ordinary people control the elected elites through referendums. A similar ideal was proposed by Machiavelli in *Discorsi*, where he noted that the Roman republic was kept 'free and powerful' because of the tension between the populace and the elite (1994, 96). Yet it was Rousseau who refined the model. In his ideal, 'each man should not be at liberty to propose new laws at pleasure [rather] this right should belong exclusively to the magistrate'. But the 'people should be giving its consent to such laws' (Rousseau 1964, 114). As I have written at length elsewhere (Qvortrup 2003), Rousseau proposed that the people, through referendums, were given a veto over proposals put forward by the 'elected aristocracy'.

Populists and the elitist backlash

In the 1890s and the two decades following saw the emergence of an American movement which was later known as 'the populists'. Like the Levellers in England in the 1640s, with whom they shared a great deal, the populists did not constitute a uniform group, nor were there eminent philosophical minds and great theorists among their number. Rather, the populists were practitioners and 'ordinary' citizens who were concerned about the growing influence of wealthy businessmen over the democratic process. Madison and others, they felt, had not adequately anticipated that both chambers of the legislature would fall prey to the influence of interest groups and lobbyists, let alone that the entire system could be captured by organised political parties with financial backers. Hence, their faith in purely representative democracy gradually declined because legislatures, while enacting laws that favoured the organised interest groups and the party machine, proved unwilling to consider legislation supported by the vast majority of the voters.

This problem was particularly acute in California, where the Southern Pacific Railroad enjoyed a monopoly of political influence, as well as controlling the party system. The situation was described Delos F. Wilcox (1912, 50), who noted that 'the citizen of every state has seen legislature after legislature enact laws for the advantage of a few and refuse to enact laws for the welfare of the many'. The same view was expressed by one of the most prominent supporters of direct democracy, Theodore Roosevelt (later president of the USA), who argued that the 'special interests which would be powerless in a general election may be all powerful in a legislature if they enlist the services of a few skilled technicians' (quoted in Munro 1912, 60). This system could not be remedied through a Madisonian system of indirect democracy; indeed, representative democracy was itself a part of the problem. The only solution, it seemed to the populists, was the introduction of direct democracy, which they believed would mean that 'the fraudulent claims bills that slide through our legislature will be vetoed by the people, and legislative extravagance will be checked' (Magleby 1984, 21).

To by-pass the elite – and to ensure that the power of the elected representatives was checked – the populists proposed three new institutions:

- the *referendum* (which enables citizens to vote on an already enacted law if they can gather a specified number of signatures to that effect);
- the *initiative* (which enables the voters to propose and vote on legislation if they can gather a specified number of signatures to that effect); and
- the *recall* (which allows citizens to hold a referendum on whether to recall an elected politician provided a specified number of signatures have been gathered).

These institutions were not introduced all over the USA, but mainly in the Pacific states of Washington, Oregon and California, and in Arizona and Colorado.

The populists considered the introduction of the initiative and the referendum as a comprehensive means of by-passing legislatures, and some of the populists even went so far as to demand that representative democracy be replaced by the initiative, the referendum and the recall. The radical politician J. Allen Smith argued that the referendum and the initiative were attempts to 'get back to the basic idea of the old town meeting, where local measures [were] directly proposed and adopted or rejected by the people' (quoted in Magleby 1984, 20). Lars A. Ueland, a

Dakota farmer and assemblyman, was equally convinced that the initiative and the referendum would

> furnish the missing link, the means needed, to make popular self-government do its best. Programs and reforms will then come as fast as people need them . . . I would rather have the complete initiative and referendum adopted in state and nation than the most ideal political party that could be made. (Quoted in Anderson 1962, 38)

Such hopes never materialised. While the initiative and the referendum were used in the first decades after their introduction to remedy the most overt problems with representative democracy, the movement fizzled out in the 1920s (Cronin 1989). These instruments were introduced only in America, and after a few decades they fell into disuse, and were revived again only in the 1970s when anti-tax crusaders successfully used the initiative to put a provision for the abolition of property taxes (the so-called Proposition 13) on the ballot in California in 1978.

The populist movement went away once it had secured the right to propose and veto laws. Once again – in an almost Hegelian way – the ideas of democracy were countered by forces from the opposite side of the political spectrum. In Europe, under the influence of elitist theorists like Mosca and Pareto, democracy was held in low esteem, as perhaps might have been expected of men who went on to become –more or less active – supporters of fascism in Italy.

What was perhaps more surprising was that generally democratically oriented writers like Schumpeter and Josè Ortega y Gasset (a Spanish liberal who opposed Franco) turned against direct governance by the people. In his influential *La rebellión de las masas* (1937), Ortega y Gasset attacked the 'triumph of hyperdemocracy (*hiperdemocracia*) in which the masses act directly' and lamented that the 'mass believes that is has the right to impose and give force to notions born in a café' (ibid., 79). Instead he defended the traditional system under which 'democracy was tempered by a generous dose of liberalism and enthusiasm for law' (ibid.).

These views persisted in the aftermath of the Second World War. The victory (in the West) of democratic countries like the USA and Britain did not lead to a revival of democratic sentiment. Political sociologists and the new breed of political scientists were, rather, sceptical of social movements and participatory democracy. Writing in the late 1950s and the early 1960s, Neil Smelser – a student of the functionalist sociologist Talcott Parsons – dismissed social movements as irrational forms of 'collective behaviour' in response to 'strain', often entailing pathological disturbances of the 'value system' (Smelser 1962, 1).

Contemporary democracy: voters, participants and the human condition

The ink was barely dry on the paper before Smelser's negative view was countered by a dramatic increase in the number of social movements, which seemed anything but pathological. The anti-Vietnam War protests in the 1960s and the environmentalists from the 1980s and onwards arguably shifted the focus. The proponents of direct democracy were once again in the ascendancy. Radical participationists like Carole Pateman, C.B. Macpherson and Benjamin Barber proposed new schemes for public engagement. As Barber wrote in *Strong Democracy: Participatory Politics for a New Age:*

> Only direct participation – activity that is explicitly public – is a completely successful form of civic education for democracy. The politically edifying influence of participation has been noted a thousand times since first Rousseau and then Mill and de Tocqueville suggested that democracy was best taught by practicing it . . . Of course when participation is neutered by being separated from power, then civic action will only be a game and its rewards will seem childish to women and men of the world; they will prefer to spend their time in 'real' pursuit of private interests. (1984, 235–236)

This view – that democracy is more than a socially useful tool for improving social conditions (as argued by utilitarians and proponents of 'protective democracy') – was not confined to democratic theorists, but was also a central theme in the philosophy of Hannah Arendt, who argued in *The Human Condition* (1958) and *On Revolution* (1963) that participation in politics can be seen as the highest form of human activity. Human beings, argued Arendt, did not exist merely to labour for a living; nor was artistic craftsmanship (work) the highest ideal. The highest form of human endeavour or action, she argued, was political engagement (Arendt 1958), because 'human action, like all strictly political phenomena, is bound up with human plurality' (Arendt 1983, 61), i.e. one should endeavour to actualise one's potential as a rational individual and a *zoon politicon* (literally, 'political animal') among our fellow citizens. According to Arendt, therefore, to be political is not *primarily* about talking, voting and fighting to improve material conditions – although those too – but about gaining recognition, acquiring a voice: 'For political freedom, generally speaking, means the right to be a participator in government or it means nothing' (1963, 218).

Some would – perhaps with justification – question Arendt's notion of the political as overly idealistic and argue that her ideal of the political being presumes rather too much of ordinary citizens. Indeed, it can – and will be – argued (see below) that too much participation drains citizens of their civic reserves. However one sees Arendt's arguments, it seems that the debate about democracy somehow has come full circle: we have returned to where we started, namely the Greek ideal of the *polis*. Arendt would have been in agreement with the great Pericles, who observed in the Funeral Oration (see above): 'Unlike any other nation we regard the citizen who takes no part in these duties [of governing the city] not as unambitious but as useless' (quoted in Thucydides 1951, 105).

Whether we agree with Arendt or Pericles – or whether we prefer Schumpeter's view that democracy is the competitive struggle for votes – is a matter that we can decide on only after careful study. It is hoped that the following chapters will provide at least a preamble to the requisite analysis.

But whatever we believe, it is perhaps worth bearing in mind that both sides in the argument – participationists and elitists – are members of the democratic family, and that they therefore agree with Haemon, in Sophocles's *Antigone*, that 'it is no polis if it takes orders from one voice' (quoted in Crick 1986, 21).

Part II

Empirical foundations of citizen politics

Having outlined the theoretical aspects of studying politics and the history of the philosophical thinking on the subject I turn now to the empirical study of citizen politics. I do so by dividing citizen engagement into two distinct categories:

- activities involving voting; and
- other civic/political activities.

In both cases what we seek to discern are the factors that determine political engagement and activity.

In chapter 3 I survey basic tendencies for which there is empirical data, including young people's alleged political apathy. Chapter 4 considers various issues in protest politics, in particular terrorism, and in chapter 5 I look at how citizens might be engaged through means other than voting in elections (e.g. through e-democracy, citizens' juries and, above all, designer politics). Discussion then turns, in chapter 6, to electoral politics and the various theories of why people vote and why they vote as they do; consideration is also given to class voting and the influence of the press on the outcome of elections.

Part II concludes with an excursus on the powers of members of Parliament (MPs). Traditional political thinking in the UK – and related countries such as Australia, New Zealand and Canada – has always maintained that British democracy, in the words of the constitutionalist L.S. Amery (1964, 1), is one of 'government of the people, for the people, with, but not by the people'. It follows from this ideal of representative government that Parliament is a strong institution which, it is supposed, can hold the executive effectively to account. Yet, while often assumed by politicians and pundits alike, this is far from always the case. Before accepting this view of Amery and others we need to consider – in some detail – the actual powers of the people's representatives. Hence Part II is concluded by a case study of Parliament in the UK.

3

An empirical approach to citizen politics

Citizen politics

Once upon a time British democracy was a beacon to the rest of the world, a shining example to be emulated. Gabriel Almond and Sydney Verba wrote of the British political scene in the 1960s:

> The participant role is highly developed. Exposure to politics, interest, involvement and a sense of competence are relatively high. There are norms supporting political activity, as well as emotional involvement in elections and system effect. And the attachment to the system is a balanced one: there is general system pride as well as satisfaction with specific government performance. (1963, 455)

Some thirty years later, the House of Commons Select Committee on Public Administration took a radically different view when it concluded:

> Not since the extension of the suffrage in 1818 has there been such a low level of participation in the electoral process. The reasons for it may be debated, but not its seriousness for our democracy. We find it extraordinary that this collapse in electoral participation, put alongside other evidence on civic disengagement, has not been treated as a civic crisis demanding an appropriate response. (2001–2002a)

Has Britain really changed that much? Are there still elements of truth in Almond and Verba's assessment or was it based on a superficial analysis? This chapter argues that – paradoxically – both assessments are, albeit in different ways, correct.

We are citizens, but we are also subjects. We are ultimately the authors of our own laws, but we are also bound by the laws of the land. We have a right to participate, but we also have responsibilities for maintaining the political system (by attending school, paying taxes and by serving as jurors, for example). It has become common to hear people decry the crisis of democracy. The seemingly relentless drop in the turnout rates in parliamentary elections is met with almost universal lamentation – not least by the press. This is not surprising perhaps: gloom sells newspapers! As any journalist will tell you, there is little mileage is in good news.

Are matters as dire as the doomsayers would have us believe? Not necessarily. There are other forms of participation than voting in elections. Political participation is a broad category which covers sundry activities, such as signing petitions, grassroots activism, being a member of the local PTA, going on strike, writing letters to the local press or hurling stones at the police in mass demonstrations. Voting is but another in this list of activities – albeit the one that is most often connected with the political debate.

Political participation has been defined as 'those legal acts by citizens that are more or less directly aimed at influencing the selection of government personnel and/or the actions they take' (Verba, Nie and Kim 1978, 1). This list seems too restrictive, and while it covers voting, campaign activity (e.g. canvassing for a local parliamentary candidate), and communal activity (attending meetings in the community), it is questionable if the word 'legal' is essential. Indeed, *illegal* mass protest (or participation in demonstrations) is often politically significant: who would claim that the mass protests against the communist regimes in Eastern Europe in 1989 were apolitical or that the race riots in Sydney in 2005 were devoid of political content?

A definition of political participation, if it is to be considered adequate, must cover all actions aimed at influencing decision-making and elite selection in a society (Shi 1997, 21). We might call all these forms of activities, for want of a better term, 'citizen politics'. Yet, even this word is problematical, as not all political participants are citizens. The riot at the Yarls Wood, a UK asylum centre, in 2002 was undoubtedly protest politics, yet the participants were not, by definition, citizens of Britain.

However, a list of activities tells us little about the political significance of different forms of participation. To understand the nature of citizen politics such activities must be put in context. Sometimes political participation is spontaneous, at other times it is not. We can – to simplify matters – distinguish between elite and citizen-initiated politics.

Some forms of participation are aimed at achieving radical changes in society (e.g. May Day protests against global capitalism in London in 2000); others are directed towards maintaining the status quo (the Countryside Alliance's mass rallies in support of fox-hunting). Political participation can take one of two forms: it is either *reformist* or *static*. Further, it can be instigated by an elite or initiated by citizen action (see table 3.1). Needless to say, this categorisation can become crude and overly simplified. However, as a rough guide, simplifications serve the heuristic purpose of making a complex reality a little more accessible.

Table 3.1 Types of citizen political participation

Elite-initiated: reformist	Citizen-initiated: reformist
Elections, which yield a mandate for change of hitherto existing policies).	Demonstrations *against* the current system or its policies.
Example: the British general election in 1945, citizens' juries, consultations.	*Example*: demonstrations against the war in Iraq in 2003.
Elite-initiated: static	**Citizen-initiated: static**
Elections or referendums, or other government-initiated forms of participation, which maintain *status quo* polices and the leadership.	Mass protest in defence of the existing system.
Example: the Australian referendum on the monarchy in 1999.	*Example*: the mass-demonstrations against the abolition of fox-hunting in 1999.

In what follows I use this model as a point of reference – although (as will become clear) it is sometimes the case that complex issues defy neat categorisation. As Walter Bagehot (2001, 7) observed: 'The genius of great affairs abhors nicety of division.'

The empirical study of citizen politics

As students of citizen politics we wish to understand both *when* citizens participate in politics and *why* they so involve themselves. Students of participation seek to understand *what* determines turnout, participation, and various forms of social protest. Some believe that political institutions can increase turnout (e.g. that electoral laws might have an impact on turnout), while others consider that cultural factors play a role, and yet others see citizen politics as a result of social factors (e.g. a higher level of education may lead to greater political participation).

Any assessment of political participation must be based on evidence rather than speculation – although the latter may inspire us in our search for the former. Political sociologists have undertaken their quest for this evidence using a variety of techniques, above all quantitative surveys. Among the most comprehensive are the topic papers published by the World Values Survey, which question samples from most countries around the world about their attitudes. Another ambitious survey is the *Eurobarometer* series, carried out among member countries of the European Union. Both surveys indicate that the British are fairly active participants, their activities being roughly comparable with those of other large EU countries such as France and Germany (see table 3.2).

Table 3.2 Citizen activities in three EU member countries

Activity	France (%)	Germany (%)	UK (%)
Sign a petition	51	55	75
Campaign activity	7	3	8
Lawful mass protest	31	25	15
Unlawful protest	10	2	8

Sources: *World Value Survey* 1990; Dalton 1998.

Some of these figures speak for themselves; others call for detailed commentary. The British are considerably more likely to sign petitions than are the Germans and the French (75 percent have done so while the figures for France and Germany are, respectively, 51 and 55 per cent). The British are fairly active in political campaigns, but rather unlikely to participate in mass-protests. While less than 20 per cent of all British respondents have been engaged in mass protests (demonstrations) almost one-third of all French citizens had been engaged in peaceful protest. Further, one in ten of the French respondents had been involved in illegal political action.

There are undoubtedly cultural reasons for this pattern. The French political scene is shaped by the cultural mythology of mass protest. Protest is integral to the way that French activists see themselves; it is perhaps indicative that two of the most quoted works in in French political philosophy in the twentieth century were George Sorel's *Reflections on Violence* (1950) and Albert Camus's *L'homme revolté* (1950). The low level of campaign activity in Germany also might be associated with historical and cultural factors. Writing in the 1960s American political scientists Almond and Verba found that Germany lacked a *civic culture* with participatory elements, whereas Britain, due to its history, had the requisites for a stable democracy. Such factors are important, yet they can be overstated.

The figures do not point to Britain as a haven of political tranquillity. The number of British citizens who have engaged in unlawful protests is almost as high as that of France in spite of the fact that British political culture does not value mass protest and civic unrest. Perhaps this is an indication that American travel writer Bill Bryson had a point when he once refereed to Britain as 'a theme-park with riots'.

But why do citizens become involved in politics? What motivates them? One factor emphasised by some political sociologists is that social class and educational background determine civic political activity. Others believe that political attitude or membership of organisations is responsible for engagement in citizen politics. Yet political activity can also be a result of dissent.

Table 3.3 Predictors of voting turnout in the UK

Variable	Value
Education[a]	.04
Party identification[b]	.24
Gender[c] (male)	−.01
Political orientation[d]	.08
Political satisfaction[e]	−.02
Age	−.24
Union membership[f]	.10

Notes: [a] years of education; [b] 2 = strong, 1 = weak, 0 = non-identifier;
[c] 1 = male, 0 = female; [d] 1 = Left, 0 = Right; [e] 1 = satisfied, 0 = unsatisfied;
[f] member = 1; R = .36 (*World Value Survey 1990*).

Measuring political participation

'There are three kinds of lies: lies, goddamn lies and statistics', the American author Mark Twain is reported to have said. He had a point. Politics is not an exact science. We can never be certain about social or political causation. Political science and political sociology seek to establish what is *probable*, not exact numbers. Yet this does *not* imply that we can entirely discard quantitative measures and statistics, for political participation can be measured statistically.

In the tables I look at the *probability* that particular groups engage in a range of different activities. The higher the figure, the greater the relationship. Thus there is a high correlation between being well-educated and taking part in demonstrations, and a positive correlation between being male and taking part in violent protests (Table 3.3). Using this approach we can answer the 'why' question in the study of political participation. While such techniques are never foolproof and should be treated with caution they can nevertheless provide valuable insights if their results are adequately analysed in the light of contextual and cultural data. Table 3.3 shows the relative effects of the chances of turning out to vote in the United Kingdom.

To the untrained eye this model may appear mystifying and complicated. While the mathematical formula underlying the model might be daunting for the uninitiated, the figures are comparatively easy to analyse – though the interpretation of them might not be beyond dispute. First, however, a word on how to analyse the data.

The statistical method used is a so-called regression model. The figures are so-called beta coefficients (often indicated by the Greek letter β), which measure the impact of each variable in a multiple regression model (for a detailed description of the technique see Lewis-Beck 1993). The table measures the statistical probability (or 'chance') that a citizen from one of the seven categories turns out to vote (in a general election). A high figure means that there is a high probability, while a low value, including a negative one, means that the probability is low or negative (e.g. being politically satisfied decreases the chances of engaging in protest (–.02). The highest possible value is 1 and the lowest is –1.

In recent years, turnout in general elections in the UK has dropped (see chapter 6). Politicians and pundits alike have pondered the reasons for this, and have considered ways of reversing this trend (see the section on postal voting in chapter 11). But how much use are these mechanisms if they fail to consider the determinants of low turnout?

Box 3.1 *Voters' engagement among black and minority ethnic groups*

One of the issues not covered in depth in the European Value Survey is the representation of black and minority ethnic (BME) groups. With generally lower levels of education and income, it is perhaps not surprising that members of BME groups are among the most *functionally disenfranchised* citizens in the UK. According to the Electoral Commission (2002c) members of the Afro-Caribbean communities especially have very low turnouts (50 per cent), with Asians slightly higher: 'Only around 50 per cent of Black and Asian voters claimed they had always voted compared with 70 per cent of whites'

As if these figures are not enough, the race riots in Bradford and Oldham in 2001, provide additional – and disturbing – evidence of public disenchantment among (especially young) ethnic minorities (Pattie, Seyd and Whiteley 2004, xvii).

While it is theoretically tempting to blame this low level of participation on traditional sociological factors, it is noteworthy that a large proportion of the respondents claim that their abstention is the result of the low number of BME candidates. This might, in part, explain why the Labour Party has done rather well among the BME voters. With more than 11 per cent of all candidates from BME communities in 2001, the party provided those citizens with the opportunity to vote for one of their own.

However other factors might also play a role, especially that the Labour Party has been perceived to be more supportive than the other parties of BME communities needs (Saggar 2000). There is, however, anecdotal evidence to suggest that this might change for some ethnic groups. While the Afro-Caribbean community still supports Labour, the Asian voters in the 2005 election shifted to the Liberal Democrats (who opposed the war in Iraq).

In some ways, the figures break with what has traditionally been assumed in political sociology. Based on predominately US data, we have come to believe that education (and hence also wealth) is the main determinant of voting in elections. According to Dalton (2002, 50) the β variable for this is .76 in the USA. In Britain – for reasons to be discussed shortly – this tendency is almost absent: its β variable is a mere .04. There is a very modest – that is to say an almost non-existent – relationship between education and electoral participation: whereas people in the US with lesser educational attainments tend to be what we might call *functionally disenfranchised*, the reverse seems to be true in the UK.

One factor that does seem to have a considerable impact on electoral participation is *age*: here the figures show a strong correlation. In other words the older you are the more likely you are to vote. This figure seems to be consistent with data suggesting that young people are functionally disenfranchised. In a report published online by the independent Power Inquiry (2006), evidence suggests that young people's participation rate is less than half of that of other adults. Such figures have been interpreted as a threat to the long-term viability of our democracy. It is, indeed, a problem if today's young people are disengaged from political matters, but it does not follow that they are destined to remain disinterested in electoral politics. Rather, it is possible –as we shall see – that interest in electoral politics grows with age.

It is perhaps not surprising that electoral participation is correlated with party attachment. As we shall see in chapter 6, voters can be divided into those who feel emotionally attached to a political party (so-called 'party identifiers') and those without party-political attachments. The party identifiers – for a number of psychological reasons – are (as the figures indicate) more likely to vote (.24), as are those who are members of a union (though the figure here is less impressive at .10).

Anecdotal evidence, and the occasional newspaper headline, suggest that growing dissatisfaction with the political system is transforming into political apathy and cynicism. The figures, however, do *not* suggest that. There is only a very modest (.02) correlation between satisfaction with the political system and turnout. In other words, those who vote are neither more nor less satisfied with democracy. The same, however, is less true for Left–Right support. In most other developed capitalist societies there is no correlation between political views on the Left–Right scale and participation (Dalton 2002, 50). In Britain there is a tendency for those on the Left to be marginally more likely to vote than those on the Right. Again, one should not throw caution to the winds of dispassionate analysis. We must always ask questions of the data: when were the figures collected and what was the context at the time?

In the case of the 2001 election the figures were collected at the nadir of Conservative support and at a time of unprecedented support for the Labour Party. This might explain why those on the Left were more likely to vote. People tend to support a winner, in politics as elsewhere. But elections – as it will be reiterated in what follows – are not the only means of political participation; they are merely the tip of the proverbial iceberg.

The fact – it can be described as nothing else – that turnout in Britain is falling does not mean that citizens have become apathetic. Comparing data from 1984–1985 and 2001, Pattie, Seyd and Whiteley found that while turnout had dropped other forms of participation had increased:

> [The] earlier data reveal that a majority of the public had voted and signed a petition, but other forms of participation were limited to small minorities. Between one in five and one in ten had contacted various people in official positions, while fewer than one in ten had engaged in various forms of direct action. What is noticeable is the considerable rise in the use of boycotts as a political action between the two time points; whereas only one in twenty acted in such a manner in the 1980s, now one in three take such action. (2004, 80–81)

There are several ways of interpreting these figures. But one possibility is that citizens need outlets for their political frustrations, and that they had to resort to other means as the parties' ideologies were so uniform that they did not offer a choice. Put differently, it made political sense to vote in the 1980s when Labour and the Tories were worlds apart ideologically – but not in 2001 and 2005 when the parties – their own protestations notwithstanding – were proponents of the same version of (social) capitalism.

Community activity, protests and sundry other civic activities arguably have political aspects too. To determine if the social background variables account for a propensity to engage in politics, we must consider those activities before we can draw any conclusions regarding the causes of political engagement.

Communal activity involves things like organising a petition drive or taking part in a community meeting. Are there differences in this area too? It used to be the case that party attachment was correlated to communal activity. Based on figures from the *Eurobarometer* survey of 1992 the figures suggest that campaign activity was associated with the citizens' attachment to a political party ($\beta =.15$). This makes sense: people join political parties because they are interested in politics and willing to give up their free time in pursuit of the policies that their party advocates.

Table 3.4 Predictors of communal activity

Variable	Value
Education	.15
Age	.07
Gender (male)	.06
Party attachment	.02
Union attachment	.10
Political satisfaction	−.01
Left–Right	.02

Note: $R = .23$
Source: *European Social Survey* 2002.

It seems almost self-evident, therefore, that these people were the more likely to be engaged in campaign activities. However, ten years later, the picture has changed. Now party attachment is no longer a predictor of communal participatory activity: those who involve themselves in such activity are neither more nor less likely to be attached to a political party.

As so often before we cannot find evidence that unequivocally explains this trend. A possible explanation could be that membership of the political parties has become less common (Mair and van Biezen 2001). Further, those who are members of the political parties tend to be older (often over 60 years of age), and hence less likely to be engaged in community activity: IVF treatment notwithstanding, the chance that you are a member of the PTA is rather small if you are over 60!

This is not the only change to have been recorded. Those engaged in community activity in 2002 were also less likely to be educated than used to be the case. In 1992 education was a strong predictor of engagement in communal activity ($\beta = .24$). To be sure, education is still a strong predictor ($\beta = .15$), but not as strong as it used to be. There may be different reasons for this, but one charitable interpretation could be that opportunities for social and political inclusion have increased through new forms of participation (e.g. citizen juries) and that this has resulted in the inclusion of those previously disenfranchised from the political process.

That union membership has a positive effect on citizens' involvement in political activity was not always the case. In the past, considerably larger numbers of individuals were members of trade unions. In part because employers could refuse to hire employees who were not unionised (the so-called 'closed shop') members of trade unions were no more politically active than their fellow-workers (Dalton 2002, 53).

To be a member of a union prior to the 1980s was not a manifestation of political orientation but part and parcel of being a worker. This has changed since the 'reforms' of the trade union laws that were carried out during the Thatcher Governments in the 1980s. It is since that time that union membership has been associated with political interest. Nowadays people who become members of unions are more likely to be engaged in communal participatory activity.

It used to be a truism that younger people are more likely to participate in political protests than are older citizens. This was certainly true to judge by the figures from the 1992 *Eurobarometer* survey. According to this study, age and protest activity were inversely correlated, i.e. the younger you are the more likely it is that you will engage in protest activities ($\beta = -.19$). This would seem to make sense: The James Dean movie *Rebel Without A Cause* was *not* about old-age pensioners! Yet, it has been suggested that the generations that were involved in the student protests in the 1960s and the 1970s would continue their habit of taking to the streets to voice their concern and occasional outrage. While the current figures (as reported in table 3.5) suggest that appetite for protest declines with age, it seems that the negative correlation between age and protest has become less pronounced. According to recent figures, the negative correlation between the two variables is now a mere –.10. What is responsible for this decline is a matter for discussion, but it seems plausible that it can be explained in part by the fact that the 'baby-boomer' enthusiasm for radical protest was not diminished due to their advancing years.

It has traditionally been assumed that demonstrations and other forms of protest politics are a last resort for the under-privileged. Assuming that those with more education are economically better off

Table 3.5 Predictors of protest politics in the UK

Variable	*Value*
Education	.12
Age	.10
Gender	.19
Union attachment	.07
Confidence in Parliament	.03
Left–Right	.17

Note: $R = .35$.
Sources: *European Values Survey* 1999–2002.

and generally privileged, it seems interesting that the level of education is a rather strong predictor of political involvement in citizen politics. That is, the more educated an individual is the higher the probability that he or she becomes engaged in political protests (β =.12). Why is that? One explanation could be that there has been a move away from traditional politics dealing with materialistic issues (such as social welfare, housing etc.) towards so-called 'post-materialist' issues, such as factors affecting the quality of life (Inglehart 1977).

An understanding of the latter requires a modicum of technical knowledge about ecology, global warming and green-house gasses, which individuals with a higher education are more likely to have. Hence the tendency that more educated people are more active in protest politics. Consequently, it would seem, demonstrations are not the domain of the under-privileged but are likely to be that of the better educated. Again, it is to be emphasised, politics is *not* an exact science.

While there are only small differences between the sexes' levels of participation in elections and communal activities, it is perhaps note-worthy that males tend to be more engaged in protest than are females (β = 19). Some psychologists no doubt see men's tendency to be engaged in unlawful protests as an indication of the greater aggressiveness of males – a view not easily substantiated. Another – more sociological – explanation would be that men more generally are employed in the man-ufacturing sector which has a tradition for unlawful protests and a higher level of unionisation. Hence the chances that men are engaged in protest activities are greater. This interpretation is supported to a degree by the slight correlation between unionisation and political protest.

What may be more surprising is that the least satisfied (measured as having least trust in Parliament) are neither more nor less likely to be engaged in protest (β = –.03). Dissatisfied citizens do not give up on pol-itics because they are dissatisfied; rather, they participate. This finding is not specific to the UK: a similar tendency can be detected in France, where the figure is –.09. In Germany political dissatisfaction is even more strongly associated with political protest (–.11), perhaps because the survey was carried out in the years of the conservative Government headed by Helmut Kohl, when the Green Party and other civic groups saw no alternative but to engage in mass demonstrations against nuclear energy (Dalton 2002, 50).

Excursus: apathetic young people?

Politics I don't really know much about it . . . But I think it is stupid that they go into it [the war in Iraq] and that people eat at McDonalds because

54 *Empirical foundations*

they do a lot of bad things to the environment. (Nina, 13, London)

Politics sucks! Boring! I couldn't be arsed. (Lachlan, 15, London)

We have no guarantee that these statements are representative, yet there is statistical evidence to suggest that they are not far off the mark. Surveys undertaken by the polling firm MORI and the UK Electoral Commission suggests that young people (those under 24) are politically disengaged – at least if measured by participation in elections (the traditional yardstick of political engagement). Young people are the group least likely to vote. In 2001 MORI estimated that only 39 per cent of the young voted. By contrast 70 per cent of those aged 65 or above turned out to vote in the general election that year. According to *Voter Engagement and Young People* (Electoral Commission 2002b, 2):

> Evidence suggests that young people in Britain have developed a more negative attitude to the process of elections and politics over the past decade or so. Young people today may be more cynical and less supportive of the political process than young people were in the 1990s. Unless this generation of young people becomes more civic-minded as they age, British democracy may become increasingly passive rather than active.

This is quite an indictment, and, given the figures cited above and the quoted statements with which this section began, a bleak picture of the prospects of a thriving democratic system emerges. It *is* a problem that so few young people vote. Yet, as Australian academic Clive Bean (2005, 9) has argued, 'While casting a vote for a political party is the most significant democratic act many people perform, it is far from the only act or orientation that cements a person's relationship with the political system'. That young people do not vote does not, therefore, prove that they are disinterested in politics.

As we have seen, turnout is normally a function of age: the older you get the more likely you are to vote. Moreover – as shown in the preceding section – there are forms of participation other than voting. A study by Henn, Weinstein and Wring (2002) suggests that matters might not be as dire as the Electoral Commission suggests. One of the problems with earlier studies is that they rely on quantitative surveys. While these can reveal general trends, they do not engage with the deeper aspects of young people's attitudes to politics. Consequently Henn et al. have used structured interviews and focus groups, as well as quantitative panel data, to gauge young people's attitudes (ibid., 173). They conclude:

> Contrary to the findings from many predominately quantitative studies of political participation, young people *are* interested in political matters, and do support the democratic process. However they feel a sense of anticlimax having voted for the first time, and are critical of those who are

Table 3.6 People's levels of political engagement

	1	2	3	4	5
All voters: How much interest do you generally have in politics?	8.0	21.0	35.0	26.0	9.0
Young voters: How much interest do you normally have in national politics	5.6	27.8	37.9	22.1	6.6

Notes: 1 = a great deal; 2 = quite a lot; 3 = some; 4 = not very much; 5 = none.
Sources: Henn et al. 2002; *British Election Study*, Post-Election Survey, cited in Sanders *et al.* 2005.

elected to power. If they are a generation apart this is less to do with apathy and more to do with their engaged scepticism about 'formal' politics in Britain. (Ibid., 167).

This finding seems consistent with the first of the two statements quoted above: it is possible to have strong views on political issues but, at the same time feel, alienated by Politics with a capital 'P'. Yet, according to Henn et al.'s statistical data from first-time voters, a majority of young people actually have at least 'some' interest in politics (see table 3.6: levels 1–3 for young people = 71.3). Indeed, it is remarkable that a full 27.8 percent are very interested in politics.

Based on these figures it seems that the number of young people who are apathetic accounts for a mere 6.6 percent of the sample, a figure which is roughly equivalent to those who claim to have a 'great deal of interest' in national politics.

One should be wary when comparing data. While figures cannot be compared directly, the figures for the young people are not least interesting because figures from the 2002 *British Election Study* showed that young people were, in fact, marginally more interested in politics than their older fellow-citizens. According to this survey only 64 per cent of all voters had at least 'some' interest in politics. To be sure, marginally fewer young people had 'a great deal of' interest in politics, but the overall finding, according to these data, is that young people are *more* interested in politics than their elders.

Needless to say one swallow of encouraging information does not make a summer of increased participation. But it seems, on the basis of these figures, a little premature to declare that young people currently are suffering from political disengagement. Further, that more than 75 per cent of young people have taken part in some form of political action outside of school hours (according to the website www.dopolitics.co.uk, accessed 11 November 2005), suggests that it is too early to lament the fate of our system of democracy.

But, again, politics is not an exact science. The tendencies in one country, in this case Britain, need not be reflected in other polities – even when they share many of the same political and cultural characteristics.

Based on an analysis of the voters from the 2001 and 2004 federal elections in Australia, Clive Bean (2005, 10) found that young Australians, unlike their British counterparts, were *less* interested in politics than their older compatriots:

> We see a substantial difference in the proportion of young people saying they have 'a good deal' of interest in politics and the proportion of older voters expressing the same outlook. In both surveys over a third of the over 30s say they have a good deal of political interest. Among the under 30s, the equivalent proportion is around a fifth. In the 2001 data it drops further again among the under 25s to around one in seven or one in eight.

It is beyond the scope of this section to go into the details of why there was this difference in the figures. It is possible that the two elections did not consider issues that were seen as relevant to young people (Wanna 2005) or that young people in Australia simply are less interested in politics in general. This is not a question that can be answered without a close analysis of Australian politics – perhaps another proof that there is no substitute for detailed empirical fieldwork and 'thick description' in politics.

Summing up

The average citizen, stated one political strategist, 'spends a mere 12 minutes a year discussing politics' (Rick Ridder, personal communication, March 2000). There is no empirical confirmation of this assessment. Figures indicate that British citizens are fairly involved in politics. Politics does not occupy their entire lives, yet a majority votes, and significant numbers of the citizenry are engaged in campaigns, communal activities or in voicing their concerns through protests. Their involvement is explained by a variety of factors. Education is the best predictor of political activity, if not of political outlook. The increase in education has led to a growing increase in political involvement, in spite of an apparent drop in the turn-out rates since the mid-1980s. Some believe that the latter is a reason for concern, as it is prompted by political apathy, declining 'social capital' or the lessening of party loyalties. Others maintain that the drop in turn-out reflects a growing mistrust of an electoral system which enables a party to gain a majority in the House of Commons without securing a majority of the votes. Neither of these theories is flawless, but neither is without merit. Political science is not an exact science; the reasons why citizens participate are varied – though several distinct patterns can be discerned.

To be sure, figures can tell us only so much. To understand citizen politics 'from the inside' – as suggested by Hannah Arendt and others (see chapter 1), we must extend the perspective and address the less definable and more qualitative aspects of politics. An understanding of why people participate is not acquired merely by correlating figures. The correlations I have looked at in this chapter tell but one side of the story – albeit an important one. But while statistics can shed light on developments, figures can tell only part of the tale. Hence to understand the essence of political participation we must address historical, cultural and contextual factors. These questions will be addressed in chapter 4.

4

Bottom–up politics: riots and extra-parliamentary participation

Citizen politics is many things, but a major aspect of it is to speak up for oneself and one's community. In this chapter I consider a number of different forms of political engagement, all of which share the feature of being *unrelated* to representative democracy. Citizen government and involvement include a broad range of activities, legal as well as illegal, new as well as old. Having looked at various forms of dissent (from citizen protests to terrorism), I turn to the mechanisms through which the citizenry can be consulted other than the ballot box.

Citizen-initiated action

Thus far I have focused discussion on two aspects of citizen politics, those which I have called 'talking' and 'voting'. But, as I said in the Introduction, there is a third aspect: fighting. Though it is less celebrated that the other two, especially by those in power, it is important to acknowledge this third means of participating, not least because there are indications that people resort to this mainly – though not only – when their opportunities for meaningful talking and voting break down.

Thinking about the politics of violent dissent has a long history in political thought. Oscar Wilde, not normally regarded as a political thinker, noted in *The Soul of Man Under Socialism*:

> Disobedience, in the eyes of anyone who has read history, is man's original virtue. It is through disobedience that progress has been made, through disobedience and rebellion. (1997, 899)

Not everyone will agree with Wilde's statement, though Hegel's claim that 'the periods of peace are the empty pages of history' (1988, 18) shows that Wilde at least had some support from esteemed philosophical circles.

There seems to be a broad consensus that citizen participation goes beyond electing MPs and that it is always necessary to hold the powers that be to account for their actions – and their inactivity. Carter (1986, 76) has argued that while

> it is widely accepted that total resistance is justifiable against a dictator-ship, a foreign occupation or a fundamentally unjust regime, normally it is condemned if it occurs within a regime which respects the rights of the citizens and in which the government can be influenced or changed from below.

Yet there are instances – hard to define though they are – when individuals engage in extra-parliamentary politics. When they do so, we tend to prefer that they engage in peaceful protests or in what is called 'civil disobedience', i.e. in a 'public, non-violent, conscientious yet political act contrary to law usually done with the aim of bringing about change in the law or politics of the government' (Rawls 1971, 364). Civil disobedience of such a kind is related to the idea that democracy is criticism – that people disagree with their leaders, voice criticisms through formal as well as informal channels. As Norman Mailer has put it: 'When you have a great country it's your duty to be critical of it so it can become even greater' (2003, 15).

Dissent, therefore, is not necessarily a threat to the system. It is increasingly recognised that for 'many individuals and groups conventional political activity is viewed as an insufficient way to articulate their concerns in an attempt to get policy-makers to pay attention to them' (Joyce 2002, 1).

Since the late 1960s several examples of so-called 'extra-parliamentary' activity hit the headlines in the UK and abroad. Protest politics includes a number of activities of differing legality and legitimacy: demonstrations, physical obstruction, consumer boycotts, civil disobedience, petitions, riots and acts of terrorism. Examples of these activities are:

- the National Federation of the Self-Employed's policy that members should withhold VAT payment from HM Customs and Excise in 1975 (civil disobedience);
- the 1984–1985 miners' strike (demonstrations and riots against the Conservative Government's decision to close unprofitable coal mines);
- the 2000 petrol crisis (physical obstruction of petrol-filling stations in protest against high fuel duties);
- the Irish Republican Army's (IRA) bombing campaign on the British mainland from the early 1970s to the signing of the Good Friday Peace Agreement in Belfast in 1998 (terrorism);

- the Countryside Alliance's pro-fox hunting demonstrations in 1998 and 2002;
- Greenpeace's urged boycott of Norwegian products in protest against commercial whaling.

Many hypotheses have been offered to explain why citizens resort to extra-parliamentary participation. The explanations – which are not mutually exclusive – focus on low status, rising expectations, relative deprivation, social isolation, class, age, lack of political influence, political outlook and education – or the lack thereof (ibid., 34).

Explanations of political dissent have always interested social theorists and scientists. According to Aristotle, the principal reason for political dissent was an aspiration to equality, whether political or economic. Much later, Nicolló Machiavelli had a stab at an explanation in *Discorsi*, in which he concluded, on the basis of historical research, that abuse of power would

> [e]xcite in the hearts of the powerless the desire to have power, either in order to take their revenge on their enemies by taking what they have from them, or in order to acquire for themselves that wealth and those honours they see their opponents abusing. (1994, 97)

Most famously perhaps, Karl Marx and Friedrich Engels argued that dissent was a result of the competition between the haves and the have-nots (Dalton 2002, 66).

Modern social scientists have echoed, qualified and, above all, quantified these themes. Ted Robert Gurr found in the late 1960s that the

> primary cause sequence in political violence is the development of discontent [over economic differences], second the politisation of discontent, and finally the actualisation of discontent in violent political action against political objects and actors. (1970, 12–13)

Until recently it was widely assumed that direct action tended to be the preserve of the Left. As Dalton has put it: 'Unconventional action is often seen as a tool for liberals and progressives [i.e. the political left] who want to challenge the political establishment' (2002, 67).

This certainly was the case in the early 1970s (see below). Yet protest has broadened across the political spectrum and is no longer the exclusive preserve of the Left. For groups that champion liberal causes on the Left there is often a counter-movement on the Right – and vice versa. An instance of this is afforded by the *pro-choice* (pro-abortion) and *pro-life* (anti-abortion) lobbies.

While political protest – as we saw in chapter 3 – is still correlated with 'liberal' causes ($\beta = .16$ according to the European Values Survey), it is noteworthy that the media increasingly are paying attention to *radical* movements on the political right, e.g. as in the case of the Countryside Alliance which engaged in violent protests against the ban on fox-hunting in Britain in 2003.

Terrorism as political action

Political violence initiated by the people is always controversial – and, by its very essence, illegal. Max Weber, the great German sociologist, famously observed that a 'state has a legal monopoly on violence' (Weber 1918). It follows from this definition that all attempts to usurp that power are illegal – though not necessarily illegitimate!

Some political theorists, most notably the French political writer Georges Sorel, have famously argued that violence has more than instrumental functions because it affords an element of political catharsis for those engaged in it: 'Proletarian acts of violence . . . are purely and simply acts of war; they have the value of military demonstrations . . . force is displayed according to its own nature' (Sorel 1950, 115). While similar sentiments were expressed by Sorel's fellow-countryman Franz Fanon, who claimed that 'only violence pays' (1961, 61), such romantic sentiments about violence are (thankfully) confined to a minority.

One of the most frequently discussed – and controversial – aspects of political engagement (some will even call it *extra-political*) is terrorism. There is a considerable and rapidly growing body of popular literature on the subject (e.g. Crenshaw 1990; Labévière 1999). Thus far, scholarly treatments of the subject have been few and far between. As Neil Smelser – doyen of social movement studies in the USA – said in an interview:

> Terrorism has been studied remarkably little by the social scientists. Political scientists, some policy makers and a few psychologists have been the main ones to be interested in it. It's been kind of left alone by sociologists, by anthropologists and by economists, with some exceptions. The literature on it now is not very good, or not very many people go into it. It's a mystery. I don't know exactly why. But there's a lot of social science that's relevant. I mean, just think of the literature on social movements. You can't understand what's going on in the Middle Eastern countries without direct application of a lot of things we know generally about social movements. And that whole question about when does evil get perpetrated and how it gets legitimized, and so on – these are things that have been thought about by psychologists and by sociologists in various ways. So, it's moving general insights that we have about these phenomena in on the understanding of terrorism . . . The whole idea of recruitment resembles very much processes such as religious conversion, and there's a rich literature on that which comes to bear, small group processes and understanding

what goes on in these cells – you can't study the cells very well but you can make some inferences out of related social science work. Reaction to disaster, sociology of disaster, is very relevant to the old issues of warning and preparation and reaction to attack. So, as much as that book is anything, it's bringing together all these different lines of independent social science work, which throws light and helps explain something that's difficult to study directly. (http://globetrotter.berkeley.edu/people5/Smelser/ smelser-con6.html, accessed 18 March 2006)

This section is not intended as a comprehensive overview, but merely as an introduction to the sociological determinants of individuals' decisions to engage in terrorist activities.

There are many different terror organisations. Some are based on a political ideology (e.g. the Marxist–revolutionary Rote Armee Fraktion in Germany in the 1970s); others have a base in small religious cults (e.g. the Aum Shinrikyo in Japan which conducted a sarin gas attack in the Tokyo subway system in 1995); and others, like Al-Qaeda (widely believed to be responsible for the attack on the World Trade Centre in New York in 2001), are supposedly 'networked' worldwide.

Different though they may be, they share certain characteristics. Unable to achieve their goals by conventional means, terrorists attempt to send an ideological or religious message by violent means. While many politicians argue that the terror attacks in 2001 have created a whole new situation, it is worth remembering that terrorism is not a novel phenomenon; in fact, terrorism has – in one form or other – been a constant feature of politics since the dawn of history. Indeed, in Israel around 50 BCE a Jewish sect known as the Zealots used terror campaigns to force insurrection against the Romans in Judea (Josephus 1970, 246). Other examples from history include the Russian Nihilists of the 1870s, described by Dostoevsky in his novel *The Possessed* (2000), and more recently various left-wing terrorists active in the 1970s. The Islamist fundamentalists at the start of the twenty-first century are but the latest in a long line of factions seeking their goals though violence.

We can define a terrorist *action* as the calculated use of violence against non-combatants. The reader will note that this definition also covers state terrorism, such as the 2003 war in Iraq. However, 'terrorism' is usually used to describe acts by non-governmental organisations. Based on the latter assumption, it is possible to distinguish between different types of terrorist, respectively:

- nationalist–separatist (IRA);
- religious fundamentalist (Al-Queda);

- new religious (Aum Shinrikyo), and;
- social revolutionary (RAF).

Because terrorism is a multi-causal phenomenon (Smelser 2002), it is difficult to develop a simple theory to account for the emergence of terror groups or individual terrorists at particular times. In the absence of a causal theory, a case study might reveal some of the underlying aspects of terrorism.

Excursus: Northern Ireland

Terrorism is not confined to spectacular events like the 1993 attack on the World Trade Centre, 9 September 2001, the continuing attacks of suicide bombers in the Middle East and the 7 July 2005 bombings in London. Until the mid-1990s terrorism was a very real part of every-day life in the UK and Northern Ireland, due – in large measure – to the IRA's 'war' on the British mainland (McGarry and O'Leary 1995). To understand IRA terrorism it is important to understand something of the historical background.

After the partition of Ireland in the early 1920s, the Unionist major- ity of Northern Ireland was able to govern the province as a *de facto* one- party state. In doing so they arguably discriminated against the interests of the – largely Roman Catholic – nationalists. After growing tension between the two groups in the 1960s, a number of measures were intro- duced to reduce the discrimination against nationalist citizens. This led to discontent among Unionists, who resorted to violence against the nationalists. Following the destruction of more than 100 nationalist homes in 1969, the modern IRA re-emerged.

While the IRA had existed since the Irish struggle for independence, its leadership had consisted of moderates. This changed when militants assumed the leadership of the organisation and sought, through armed attacks on citizens in the province, to achieve Irish unity. When this failed to bring about the desired effect, the IRA began a bombing cam- paign on mainland Britain. Examples of this campaign include the killing of nineteen civilians in Birmingham in November 1974, the killing of several government ministers, and an almost successful attempt to kill Prime Minister Margaret Thatcher in the autumn of 1984. From the early 1970s to the mid-1990s a total of 3,600 people were killed in the conflict (1,000 more than in the 9/11 attacks!), the IRA being responsible for more than 1,800 deaths (only 465 were British sol- diers). While the IRA killed the largest number of civilians, the loyalist paramilitaries were not innocent. Over 980 civilians were killed – most of who were targeted Catholics. It is difficult, if not impossible, to explain why the IRA declared a 'complete and unequivocal cease-fire' on 31 August 1994 (a declaration reciprocated by the loyalists a month later).

Among the factors could be mentioned the IRA's failure to counter the loyalist paramilitaries' increasingly successful attacks and the dwindling public support for *armed struggle* were certainly factors. Yet it was not only the IRA who realised that the ongoing 'war' was both futile and costly. The governments of the Republic of Ireland and the UK began to reach an understanding (whereas they had previously tended to take different sides). Of great symbolic – and real – importance was the declaration by Secretary of State for Northern Ireland Peter Brooke in the early 1990s that 'Britain had no selfish, strategic or economic interest in Northern Ireland'.

The agreement of the Irish and British Governments to let the people decide effectively undermined the rationale for the armed struggle, and led to the Good Friday Peace Agreement in 1998. Fighting had given way to voting and talking! Finally, in 2005, after a period of bad press (the IRA had been accused of robbing the Northern Bank in Belfast) the republican movement declared that 'the war was over'.

Why terrorism?

But why did the IRA resort to these tactics? Sociologists have generally argued that the causes of revolution and political violence in general are also the causes of terrorism (Gurr 1970). That is, lack of peaceful communications channels – in addition to other factors (religious and ideological) create the conditions under which terrorism thrive.

The nationalist and republican minorities, i.e. the Catholics, of Northern Ireland were largely excluded from positions of influence, hence their resort to terrorism. This is a reasonable explanation that covers more than the Irish case. Indeed, a case could be made for the view that Palestinian terrorism is a result of the disentranchement of those living in the occupied territories (Esposito 2002, 23).

The case of Italian terrorism in the 1970s suggests a similar pattern. At that time Italian politics was characterised by the permanent exclusion of the radical Right (the neo-fascist party FSI) and the radical Left (the Communist Party) from government. One of the results of this was a growth in terrorism on both sides of the political spectrum.

Studying terrorism is notoriously difficult, not least as terror groups by their very nature are secretive and closed organisations. Following the arrest of terrorists in Italy and Germany in the 1980s, sociologists

Table 4.1 Prior occupational profile of Italian female terrorists, January
1970 – June 1984

Occupation prior to becoming	Number	% of total terrorists a terrorist
Clerk, secretary, nurse, technician	57	23
Criminal	5	2
Free professional	8	3
Housewife	11	5
Industrialist	5	2
Police, military	1	0
Small-business proprietor, salesperson	3	1
Student	86	35
Teacher	50	20
Worker	18	7
Total	244	100

Source: Weinberg and Eubank 1987, 250–252.

sought to understand the sources of terrorism by studying the social profile of the members. Table 4.1 shows some of the results of one of those studies (in this case the social and occupational profiles of female terrorists in Italy).

These people were not criminals prior to engaging in their terrorist activities. And while most terrorists in 1970s' Italy claimed to act on behalf of the 'proletariat' from within groups on the Left (ibid.), only 7 per cent were actually workers.

As can be seen from the table, the terrorists were predominately well-educated women (35 per cent were students), teachers (20 per cent) or women working as clerks and secretaries (23 per cent). With the possible exception of the latter category, the rest of the groups have had a disproportionately high level of political participation. The women who engaged in terrorist activities did not, therefore, belong to groups that traditionally are functionally disenfranchised. This might provide at least the outline of a theoretical explanation of the phenomenon as least as regards Italy in the 1970s. That explanation might lie in the concept of *relative deprivation*, developed by Gurr (1970) and others, according to which people experience feelings of deprivation mainly when they compare their own situations unfavourably with those of other individuals or groups.

The women who engaged in terrorism in Italy – according to this theory – felt that their influence (when compared to followers of the ruling parties) was limited. While they had considerable rights under the Constitution, they were unable to get as much influence as those who supported the centrist parties or even the radical Right; hence their use of radical means. While this explanation goes some way in explaining why some engage in terror, it still leaves many questions to be answered. Perhaps Fyodor Mikhailovich Dostoevsky, the great Russian novelist, was right when he noted,: 'While nothing is easier than to denounce the evildoer, nothing is more difficult than to understand him.'

Summing up

Political participation, as we have seen, involves more than just supporting the system by voting in government elections; it incorporates also various ways of showing dissent, whether through signing petitions, through mass protest – and even through civil disobedience. We have seen that citizens can sometimes feel *impelled* to resort to *extra parliamentary politics* when the traditional means of influencing politicians fail. Yet, while these mechanisms are often healthy ones, they can degenerate, especially if a group feels politically disenfranchised.

In these circumstances politics can turn nasty and result in violent protest – even terrorism. The terrorist's forms of participation are rarely constructive (though it should not be forgotten that some terrorist movements are later canonised, as in the case of the African National Congress in South Africa!).

Under most circumstances, however, extra-parliamentary politics is less effective than organised politics. The question, therefore, whether there are ways in which governments and citizens can engage in a fruitful dialogue to ensure that the preferences of the citizens are heard and acted upon. In the next chapter I consider some forms of citizen (re-)engagement, some based on deliberative processes (e-democracy and citizen juries) and others based on a more elitist conception of democracy (e.g. various forms of designer politics).

5

Top–down politics: e-democracy, citizens' juries and designer politics

What can governments do if the citizens are unwilling to get engaged in politics through the usual channels? In recent years the answer has been provided by two mechanisms: citizen juries and e-democracy. In addition to those mechanisms, governments, in pursuit of votes, arguably, rather than the voters' opinions, have developed methods and techniques for polling and measuring voter preferences through, for example, *focus groups*.

e-democracy

Democracy, we are often reminded, means rule of the people. Yet, at a time of declining electoral participation, the legitimacy of public policies requires more than the usual mechanisms of public engagement. This is especially the case in matters concerning the environment and physical planning, where policies have irreversible consequences. Perhaps in recognition of this, new mechanisms of public engagement have been pioneered: the British Government and MORI experimented with a 'People's Panel' from 1998 to 2002; virtual conferences on greenhouse emissions were held in Canada in 2002; and the Australian Defence Review 2000 was based the input of thousands of citizens (Coleman and Gøtze 2004).

While there was considerable scepticism regarding the scope for e-democracy in the early days (Katz 1997, 96), models of public engagement have come a long way in recent years. In the 1980s various experiments were conducted in Alaska and Hawaii with a view to increasing public participation (Becker and Scarce 1984). While the initial responses were favourable (Arterton 1987, 23), the experiments were often criticised for their utopian nature: e-democracy was seen as an ideal pursued by super-engaged citizens, and not as a serious contribution to increasing public participation.

This has changed. Practical experiments in a host of different countries have shown that e-participation can – when done with care –

improve both policy-making and increase legitimacy. Not everybody wants to be engaged all the time and on all issues. Nor do they need to be. By utilising the mechanisms developed in, for instance, marketing, it has proved possible to target those stakeholders who are most likely to be affected by a particular policy (Levine, Fung and Gastil 2005). The Queensland Government has come up with what appears to be the most 'joined-up' Australian response to e-democracy, outlining an ambitious three-year initiative. The policy statement reads:

> The Internet is not inherently democratic, but it can be used for democratic purposes . . .The strengths of this new technology are many. The characteristics of the Internet which support e-democracy include: timeliness – the opportunity to participate in debates as they happen; accessibility – participation is less limited by geography, disability or networks; and facilitation – individuals and groups can access information and provide input which previously has often been restricted to organisations which had the resources to respond to government. (www. premiers.qld. gov.au/about/community/pdf/edemocracy, accessed 17 March 2005)

But these are the success stories. More often than not, public-engagement exercises fail to ignite the public's attention. Anecdotal evidence suggests that while thousands of pounds are spent on electronic consultations, only a handful of people log on to the specially designated websites. Further there is evidence to suggest that white middle-class professionals are participating more than other groups (Norris 2001). While this is often true for other forms of civic engagement, the tendency is more pronounced in e-consultations (ibid.). For the sake of consistency, it might be useful to adopt an approach similar to the one used to measure the determinants of participation among different groups (see chapter 3).

Table 5.1 Predictors of internet activity

Variable	*Value*
Age	−.03
Gender (male)	.58
Education	.78
Income	.30
Class	.82

Note: R = .94.
Sources: *EuroBarometer* 44; Norris 2004.

Compared to the other figures of participation reported in chapter 3 it is evident that the internet is used significantly more by those with higher education (β = .78) and by those of the upper classes (β = .82). Use of the internet is also heavily biased in favour of males (β = .58) and to a certain extend those of the higher income brackets (β = .30). Perhaps predictably, there is a slight tendency for younger citizens to use the internet a little more than their elders, though this tendency is very modest indeed (β = –.03). Generally, however, these figures are extremely high.

While it is obviously problematical to extrapolate from internet use to potential participation in e-democracy, the indications are that the internet is likely – at least for the time being – to further increase the participatory disparities among citizens. Based on these figures, Pippa Norris concluded:

> If remote voting, via computer terminals in the home or workplace, were introduced into UK elections within a few years . . . the digital divide will probably reinforce, or even widen, many of the familiar socioeconomic disparities in electoral participation that already exist, including those of class, education, gender and income. (2005, 5)

This insight was not lost on the late Italian philosopher Norberto Bobbio, who presciently warned against the coming of a *computer-crazia* in his book *Il futuro della democrazia* (*The Future of Democracy*), originally published in 1984 (1995, 34). This was not a welcome prospect, and is, indeed, a reason for reconsidering the case for an ever growing citizen involvement. Many reformers stress the edifying consequences of participation as ends in themselves (Barber 1984, 236). But it seems difficult to maintain this support for increased opportunities for participation if they reinforce already existing democratic inequalities.

This was observed also by an earlier generation of political scientists, including Gabriel Almond, Sidney Verba and Robert A. Dahl. They predicted that schemes of direct participation would place excessive demands on citizens which would drain their 'civic reserves'. Too much participation, they argued, would create democratic fatigue. In their view, by limiting participation to periodic elections, referendums and occasional civic protests the citizens could save their political energies for *really* important issues. Alfred Hirshman has summed up the view:

> The ordinary failure, on the part of most citizens to use their potential political resources to the full makes it possible for them to react with unexpected vigour, by using normally unused reserves of political power and influence, whenever their vital interests are threatened. (1970, 32)

Yet it is still early days for e-democracy. Perhaps once citizens have learned to use the internet the conclusion will be otherwise. Enthusiasts for e-democracy have sounded an altogether more optimistic note by observing that the internet provides – for the first time – opportunities for genuine two-way communication between the governors and the governed. As Morris has noted:

> The essence of the Internet is that it permits you to speak, that it makes monologue into dialogue . . . the message of the media of the internet is interactivity and dialogue, and that enforces a discipline on the sender of the communication which is called customisation and responsiveness, and it will totally change the method by which we govern, by which we run for office, by which we lobby those who are in office. (2003, 15)

But it is difficult to resolve this debate through dispassionate analysis. Whether one accepts Hirschman's view or the opposite position seems to depend on one's philosophical outlook, or, as Peter McLaverty has put it, your 'approach will depend upon what you think is desirable for individuals and or for society' (2002, 194).

Citizens' juries

There are many buzz-words in politics. A recent one – at least at the time of writing – is the 'citizens' jury'. Based on the distinction outlined above, a citizens' jury is an example of an elite-initiated reformist strategy. Pioneered in the USA in the 1970s, citizens' juries began to be used in the UK and Australia in the 1990s, especially by the Labour Party (Carson 2004). Within 4 years of the election of New Labour in 1997 over 100 juries had deliberated in the UK on issues as diverse as Northern Ireland, educational reforms, health rationing, waste disposal and genetic testing. Many of the academics, local authorities and non-governmental agencies who led this first wave of experiments based their enthusiasm on the supposed potential of citizens' juries to combine citizen deliberation, the interrogation of specialist evidence and participatory approaches to problem-solving (Smith and Wales 2000).

Like a legal jury, a citizens' jury is based on the idea that once a small sample of a population has heard the evidence, its subsequent deliberations can fairly be taken to represent the conscience and intelligence of the community. Juries are rarely studied by political theorists today (though see Carson 1999), but this was not always so. In his seminal *De la démocratie en Amérique*, Alexis de Tocqueville noted that 'to regard the jury simply as a judicial institution would be taking a very narrow view of the matter . . . The jury is above all a political institution' (1988,

272). This is so, argued Tocqueville, 'because there is always a republican character in it, in as much as it puts real control of affairs into the hands of the ruled, or some of them, rather than into the hands of those of the rulers' (ibid., 272).

Members of a citizens' jury are given time to reflect and deliberate freely with each other (though they may occasionally be assisted by a neutral advisor), as well as opportunities to scrutinise the information they receive from witnesses, whom they interrogate themselves.

We have seen that one of the problems with mass democracy today is that the level of participation generally is higher among those who are well-educated and the middle classes. Citizens' juries are – in part – intended to compensate for this by providing a supplementary way of ensuring that marginalised groups are properly represented. The citizens' jury, as Lyn Carson has eloquently put it, is a mechanism for 'stimulating the voice of the voiceless' (2001, 57).

The citizens' jury is not a panacea. Some observers are sceptical about its value or effectiveness as a form of consultation. Even if such juries are representative, they would not always be perceived as such, and opponents in a debate will always find arguments to question the selection of the jury and seek to undermine its legitimacy. Quintin Oliver, founder and first chair of the UK-based Consultation Institute adds:

> Many dialogue methods become fashionable for a period, and the Citizens' Jury is one such technique. It falls on several counts, not least its weakness at delivering wider democratic engagement and empowerment. (Oliver, personal communication 10 March 2006)

Further, as can happen with an opinion poll, the outcome can be misleading if the issue is presented in a biased way. For example, a citizens' jury run by the Welsh Institute for Health and Social Care (WIHSC 1997), and evaluated by Dunkerley and Glasner (1998), was reportedly steered towards an answer which suited the policy preferences of the organisers.

For citizens' juries to be a mechanism of proper democratic consultation, the jurors must be allowed to interrogate witnesses and scrutinise the various sources of information. If they are merely passive recipients of written briefings and specialist testimonies, they do not serve their purpose.

Citizens' juries and other similar processes are frequently undertaken on contentious issues, and accusations of unfairness and bias have been made not only by stakeholders, but by external evaluators (Barns 2005). Such accusations are part and parcel of any system of democracy, though they can be minimised by ensuring that the process should is overseen by an advisory group composed of all relevant stakeholders (Coote and Lenaghan 1997, 79).

Do citizens' juries work? The proof that they do is probably provided by the decline in their use. Having seen that the findings of citizens' juries were often critical of government, funding for such experiments has now largely been transferred back to safer, more controllable, methods such as focus groups. Democracy is always difficult when the guardians wish to protect themselves!

Designer politics: politics by opinion polls?

Politics has changed in recent years – and will probably continue to undergo alterations – and the internet is not the only reason. Another – though less frequently discussed – phenomenon to have an impact is designer politics. This is how one practitioner–observer sees it:

> It used to be that a politician had to go by instinct and hunch in figuring out what the voters would approve or what they would take . . . But then polling came in . . . now every politician that votes on an issue knows what the poll numbers are he is voting on. (Morris 2003, 15)

All governments – and opposition parties – will seek to present their own policies in the best light possible. However, there are indications that politicians in recent years have become more aware of presentational issues –what is here called 'designer politics' – than was previously the case.

In recent years the political vocabulary has been enriched – or devalued – by terms like 'spin doctor', 'sound bite', 'focus group' and 'polling'. Tony Blair's former (1997–2003) press spokesman and director of communications Alistair Campbell, former Cabinet Minister Peter Mandelson and the PM's 'pollster' Philip Gould have been singled out as 'princes of darkness' and have been accused of manipulating public opinion. These issues are relevant for the present purposes because they are based on the idea of public consultations with voters, i.e. part of a two-way process.

What is designer politics?

In the days of class politics matters were simple in both the UK and Australia. Each political party represented a group or class in society. The parties formulated policies that were articulated by interest organisations which spoke for the ordinary members. In the cases of the UK's Labour Party and Australia's Labor Party, the policies originated from the trade unions. A high proportion of citizens at that time were members of political parties. In short, it was then comparatively easy for political parties to formulate ideas; they could rely on their individual members and organisations. Today's political parties face different circumstances. No longer able to formulate policies on the basis of demand from ordinary party members, political parties are forced to look elsewhere for policy ideas – and for assessment of policies. Political parties can – crudely speaking – choose between two options: they can adopt an ideological stance (and hope that enough people agree with them) or they can design a policy on the basis of inputs from the electorate. The latter is what is meant by *designer politics*.

Some have argued that this means that all ideological positions and beliefs disappear from the political discourse (Barns 2005). That is not the view taken by many political consultants. According to Dahlia Scheindlin, designer politics actually enables ideological parties to determine which goals to pursue:

> My perspective [is that] there is another option, which is how I see our work: they [the political parties] can choose an ideological stance and gather the deepest possible input from the public in order to find out the best way of communicating it, and possibly the best way of refining it to meet the precise needs of the public they are trying to serve within their ideology. It's sort of a cross between the two. But this is the reality – I have never worked with a candidate/party who started with nothing and creating ideology/policy based on research – rather they start with positions and try to figure out whether they work, in order to learn how to refine them, communicate them, and at worst, develop policy ideas that will make the ideology tangible to targets likely to respond to that ideology. (Personal communication March 2006)

The remainder of this chapter looks at the anatomy of designer politics. I also attempt to trace its historical origins. While the methods, techniques and terminology has changed, designer politics has been around since the Greek *polis*.

Are media advisers manipulating public opinion? Has presentation become more important than substance? And can 'spin' lure voters? How – if at all – can public opinion be shaped? What do spin doctors do? What is designer politics?

This account and assessment of the (not so novel) phenomenon of *designer politics* draws on interviews with practitioners and examples from the (mainly American) literature. While designer politics has been studied extensively by specialists in marketing and communication (Thurber 1998, 145), the phenomenon has attracted hardly any interest from political scientists studying the determinants of elections and referendums (see, however, Lees-Marshment 2001 and 2004). As a consequence, little is known about the causes (or the effects) of the political marketing revolution.

Rhetoric and sophistry: the history of designer politics

'There is no new thing under the sun' reads an often-quoted verse from the Old Testament (Ecclesiastes 1.9). This is certainly true of designer politics. We are used to thinking that political marketing is a recent invention. We should think again. In a sense, designer politics is as old as politics it self, and it is arguably true that no democracy has ever existed without some use of political marketing – though the forms and the art have changed through time.

The Greeks and the Romans spoke of sophistry and rhetoric – today we call the same thing political marketing, designer politics and spin (Friedenberg 1999). In Athens in the fifth century BCE, the use of designer politics – and the reactions against it – was part of the political woodwork. Socrates said in Plato's dialogue *Protagoras*: 'Watch or the sophist might deceive us in advertising what he sells, the way merchants who market food for the body do' (Plato 1997, 731 [313d]) While the Athenian sophists bore little resemblance to infamous *spin doctors* of today, Protagoras's description of his activities is surprisingly modern: 'What I teach is how to realize one's maximum potential for success in political debate and action' (Plato 1997, 755 [319a]).

That no less a figure than Plato (428–348 BCE) raged against the so-called sophists, the professional teachers who trained budding politicians to convince their audiences, might be seen as a devastating critique of designer politics. Yet, Plato's misgivings do not rob sophistry or designer politics of democratic legitimacy.

Plato was famously opposed to democracy (See chapter 2). The sophists, conversely, were not. The sophists were – so it could be argued – merely helping the politicians to communicate more effectively. We find a more neutral description of rhetoric (and of democracy) in Aristotle's writings: rhetoric is described as 'the power to observe the persuasiveness of which any particular matter admits' (Aristotle 1991, 74).

The same neutral description can be found in Cicero's writings. Cicero is often revered by traditionalists. A defender of the Roman republic and democracy, Cicero defined rhetoric as 'speech designed to persuade' (www.americanrhetoric.com/rhetoricdefinitions.htm, accessed 16 March 2006). He was not alone in this. Even St Augustine was a teacher of rhetoric, though, perhaps tellingly, he gave up that career when he embraced his vocation as a Christian theologian.

That designer politics has been part and parcel of democratic politics since the dawn of this form of governance does not, however, imply that the art is equally widespread and common. While in some countries (e.g. the USA) extensive use is made of political consultants, in other countries the profession is hardly present at all

To understand *designer politics* it is necessary to take a look at what actually happens. The section following presents an overview of the key stages in a typical electoral campaign.

An anatomy of designer politics

Designer politics – in its modern form – is an American phenomenon. It is based on the premiss that it is possible to engineer policies that suit the electorate (Johnson 2001). This is a far less idealistic version of politics – one based on the Schumpeterian notion that democracy is a system under which different elites compete for the citizens' votes (Schumpeter 1951).

In designer politics – or political marketing (Lees-Marshment 2002) – this view is taken to its radical extreme: voters are treated as consumers, and the political parties – like all salesmen – are carrying out analyses and surveys to gauge what the customers think of the political wares on offer. What makes this possible? How can the parties determine the policies which really suit the voters? They do so through opinion polls and focus groups.

In the run-up to a general election a party usually conducts a benchmark poll, i.e. an opinion poll that asks the respondents for demographic information – their age, sex, location, etc. – and about their education, general political attitudes, their feeling towards the party. This poll will normally (but not always – see below) be followed up by various other polls during the campaign, the aim of which is to gauge the party's progress and to detect the public's feelings towards the continuing campaign, by checking the impact and success of that party's strategy, but also the public's responses to other developments in the general election environment.

On the basis of the benchmark poll the party seeks to identify policies that suit the electorate. Having found those policies the party tests them on small *focus groups*. A focus group is made up of (typically 6–12) voters who are asked to discuss a proposal, a poster or an idea. Sometimes the discussion is observed from behind a screen; sometimes a facilitator takes notes; and sometimes the discussion is recorded.

As noted above, some campaigners do things in a different order. As Dahlia Scheindlin explains there are good reasons for that:

> Some of us do focus groups prior to a survey, in order to allow people to talk freely and openly, with practically no guidance or closed questions, so that we can first hear as broadly as possible what's really going on. On the

basis of what arises in those groups, we conduct surveys with greater confidence that we are not dictating the kinds of questions being asked and
distorting the results. We can ask things using the terminology people use
themselves, rather than in questions designed by a bunch of politicians
that force people to agree or disagree with things they are hearing in unfamiliar ways. (Personal communication, March 2006)

The aim of the focus group is to record the public's assessment of the
policies. In Philip Gould's words the importance of focus groups is that
they enable politicians to listen directly to 'the voters' voices' (Gould
1998, 326). This is essential. It is not enough that a political party
adopts a new image which is supported by the majority of the voters.
The political party must be seen as a credible exponent of the policy. This
is not automatically the case. The British Conservative Party under
William Hague (1997–2001) sought to modernise by adopting a contemporary image. While this was consistent with the voters' preferences,
the Tories were not seen as credible delivers of the new message (Lees-
Marshment and Quale 2001).

Having gone through these two phases, the party is ready to launch
the policy. This is not straightforward. Party officials responsible for
public relations (derogatorily referred to as spin-doctors) will now seek
to feed their angle to the press. Selected journalists may be invited to
the Prime Minister's week-end retreat – *Chequers* in England or *Kiribili
House* in Australia – possibly in the hope that they will return the hospitality in the form of a positive news story.

The other party – assuming a two-party contest – will itself be busily
engaged in challenging the first party's presentation of its new policy,
typically through so-called *opposition research* (sometimes referred to as
rebuttal).

During the campaign, officials and campaign workers will compile
files and data on the other party and its policies which will be used to
rebut those policies. Rebuttal is thus a counter-attack on the opposition,
outlining the 'real' consequences and the alleged 'the hidden costs'
involved. As a political consultant explains:

> This is called opposition research (affectionately known as opp, or oppo,
> research) and also has been maligned and controversial – being called any-
> thing from 'digging up dirt' to 'due diligence', i.e. knowing the facts of the
> case . . . Opp research is a vital link for laying out the facts of the case to
> the voter, predicting the kinds of issues and attacks that are likely to be
> raised during the campaign, and preparing rebuttals ahead of time, to
> ensure rapid response – rule number one of modern campaign strategy –
> with genuine facts and not just empty rhetoric or low-level mudslinging.
> (Dahlia Scheindlin, personal communication, March 2006)

While these strategies are increasingly used it remains an open question how effective they are. Rick Ridder, past president of the *International Association of Political Consultants*, has estimated that a campaign can 'at best win up to five per cent. You cannot turn an awful candidate into a good one. You can minimize damage' (Personal communication May 2000). Whatever the effects, political parties cannot afford *not* to use these tactics: the risk that eschewing such tactics could cost them the election is too great. This clearly gives the bigger parties an edge. In Australia, smaller parties like the Greens cannot afford the expenditure on the media that the larger parties incur. Indeed, the *total* budget of one of the smaller parties is often dwarfed by the amount of money spent by the larger parties on the promotion of policies alone.

To take but one example: prior to the 1998 Federal Election, Prime Minister John Howard's Liberal Government authorised the expenditure of $16 million on a campaign promoting the introduction of a Goods and Services Tax (GST). After it had won the election it spent a further $36 million on a television advertising campaign promoting the introduction of the GST (*Sydney Morning Herald*, 30 May 2000).

Some might see this as unfair. Can we say that democracy is fair if the larger parties are allowed to advertise their policies, whereas the smaller parties are silenced because they do not have sufficient money to pay for advertising? In Britain paid political advertising is illegal. In Australia this is not the case: in 1991 the Labour Government enacted a law banning television advertisements, but the Act was struck down as unconstitutional by the Supreme Court, which found that it was incompatible with the principle of freedom of speech (Moore and Maddox 1995).

However, campaigning is more than advertising. Increasingly, the political parties are interested in the micro-targeting of voters. An example of this that has received considerable coverage is the so-called *Government Members Secretariat* (GMS) set up by the Howard Government (Barns 2005).

Based on extensive coverage of individual voters' preferences (as expressed on 'the door-step', in letters to newspapers, etc.), the Liberal Party in Australia has developed a database (called 'Feedback') which can be used by campaigning candidates (the Australian Labor Party has a similar system and a database called 'Electrac' (ibid., 15). According to political scientists Peter van Onselen and Wayne Errington (2004, 358), the system works in this way:

> [Y]ou call an electorate office to express concerns about, let's say, the recent war in Iraq. Those views are logged into the database against your

name. Caller ID technology means that even if you don't give up your name they can look it up by matching the displayed number to your address (if that is where you are calling from). Or your local MP goes door-knocking. You think he or she has randomly chosen your house to visit. Wrong. They have downloaded your information, and are coming to find out more about you, logging it against your name when they return to office . . . Ever had one of these conversations feeling that you really connected with your local MP? That is probably because before they door-knocked your house they read your data base entry, identified issues of concern to you, and peppered the conversation with references to those issues.

Political parties still need staff and volunteers to seal envelopes and deliver leaflets, though that, too, has changed in recent years. But is this 'micro-targeting' a threat to democracy? One Italian political theorist believes so. In his *Il futuro della democrazia* Bobbio warned:

> It is no longer in the in the realm of science fiction to imagine direct democracy being made possible by means of computer technology. And why should not the same computer technology make it possible for those in power with a similar detailed knowledge of our private lives, even in mass society? The knowledge that absolute monarchs such as Louis XIII or Louis XIV had about their subjects bears no comparison with what a well-organised state can obtain about its citizens . . . What a small amount of power when compared to the enormous possibilities opening up for a state which has at its disposal huge electronic brains . . . It [is] a trend completely at variance with the one which inspired the ideal of democracy as the apotheosis of visible power: it is a trend not towards the maximum control of power on the part of the citizens, but on the contrary towards the maximum control of the subjects on the part of those in power. (1995, 109–110)

Designer politics and democratic governance

Some writers believe micro-targeting to be a threat to democracy. According to Greg Barns, an Australian writer and former staffer in John Howard's office, designer politics in general – and micro-targeting in particular – is problematical because it 'essentially treats democracy as a market in which the idea is to pitch a product before the voter, knowing [his or her] every hope, aspiration, weakness, foible and fetish' (Barns 2005, 66).

Proponents, on the other hand, would argue that designer politics, far from being undemocratic, is a natural consequence of the Schumpeterian conception of democracy as 'competitive leadership' (Schumpeter 1951, 284). According to its advocates, designer politics is merely enabling the competition on the political market by helping the politicians identify the views of the citizens at a time when the political parties no longer represent the citizenry. Designer politics, according to this view, provides the link between the elite and the people, one which previously was provided by the political parties.

Some would undoubtedly prefer that this function be transferred back to the parties themselves. The parties had a socialising function, which is necessary in any democracy. Further, the members of parties took (and take) an interest in the subject of politics. Ordinary citizens do not deliberate when they are asked a couple of questions by a pollster. The use of such modern techniques is not a panacea; our system of government is not like that of Voltaire's Dr Pangloss; we do *not* live in the best of all possible worlds!

Yet modern designer politics provides the citizens with a valuable input into the political process (Lake 1989). Further, the ordinary citizens are more representative of the population as a whole. The members of political parties are likely to be more middle-class, white and urban than the population as a whole. Moreover, there is some evidence that party members are more likely to hold extremist views. As David Butler noted in a famous analysis, one which still seems accurate: the essential dilemma for party leaders is that 'their most loyal and devoted followers tend to have more extreme views than they have themselves, and to be still further removed from the mass of those who actually provide the vote' (1960, 385).

This view remains, arguably, true. Jeffrey Stonecash, a US political scientist and pollster, has recently found that 'core supporters' have 'policy preferences that tend to be either very liberal [left-leaning] or very conservative, and not moderate' (2003, 3). By relying on the views of party members – so the hypothesis goes – the parties are more likely to develop policies that are inconsistent with the views of the voters as a whole. When relying on the views of the citizens as interviewed in mass surveys and focus groups, the parties are more likely to represent a middle-of-the–road position. It is this situation, according to Stonecash, that has prompted 'politicians to use polls and focus groups to try to find a language for discussing policy proposals that will allow them to sound as if they are responding to the majority' (ibid.).

It that a good thing? Not everyone thinks so. Alistair Palmer has commented that New Labour (through its use of designer politics' tactics) is 'a populist government, whose policies are driven by polls, focus groups . . . and the next logical step is to re-introduce the death penalty for murder' (1998, 44). Yet, interestingly, that dire consequence has not materialised either in Britain or in Australia.

Moreover it is, questionable whether the introduction of illiberal – or populist – policies itself is an argument against particular political practices, such as designer politics. A political practitioner has defended modern campaign techniques on the grounds that:

> The electorate is more demanding and is right to be so. It is up to us to meet the challenge. I do not just see focus groups and market research as campaigning tools; increasingly I see them as an important part of the democratic process: part of the necessary dialogue between politicians and people; part of a new approach to politics. (Gould 1998, 328)

Or, as Dahlia Scheindlin puts it in a personal communication (2006):

> I think anyone who has ever witnessed a focus group [will agree that], there is something extremely gratifying about presenting a memo to a prime minister or PM candidate with direct quotes from a 55–year old woman from a remote area of the country who has felt far from the centres of power her whole life. I have watched from the observation room when a focus group ends and a participants says eagerly to the moderator – 'will the things we said actually go to the (candidate/leader)?' and I smile behind the glass where they can't see me or even know who i am, and say to myself – 'yes it will'.

Of course, there are other opinions, as a letter to the editor of the *Daily Telegraph* despairingly put it:

> Sir – The Power Commission concludes that the source of electoral apathy is people believing they don't have any power and are not listened to. This is a myth. The problem is that they are listened to far too much. The result, via market research, is that the average (centrist) opinion is in the policy bag of every major party. Politicians used to represent the interests of their supporters and intentionally upset large swathes of their opponents. Nowadays they all try to represent the average voter, who does not exist, but is merely a statistical construct. The Average Party is now in power, or trying to be, all the time. Boring! Even worse, it represents nobody. (28 February 2006)

It would be folly to argue that the UK's is a perfect system of democracy. It is not! Political spin and many of the things that go with it are negative and based on less than altruistic motives. But it is questionable whether the old system was as good as the nostalgic would have us believe.

To be sure the view that designer politics provides a new link between people and their representatives does sound a little too neat and a little too Panglossian, and is true only if we accept a rather minimalist definition of democracy along the lines of Schumpeter (1951, 269).

As noted above, the fact that not all parties have equal (financial) access to the media's advertising capacities is a cause for concern. But whether democracy would be served by doing away with designer politics is an open question. It seems that a system in which the preferences of the citizens are recognised is better than a system based on the views of the unrepresentative members of political parties.

Conclusion

There are no studies of the effects of designer politics. So why resort to this expensive means of convincing the voters? Commercial factors may play a role: the emergence of firms selling their know-how may have created a market. Yet the reasons may also be of a structural kind: with the decline in party membership the main political parties – increasingly divorced from the traditional hinterland of interest organisations – no longer get direct input from members and sympathisers. This lack of policy input has forced the parties to seek new ways of gauging the voters' demands and attitudes. Parties and their candidates seek to do this using public opinion surveys and focus groups. Whether this trend will prove detrimental to political participation and citizen politics remains to be seen.

6

Citizens as voters

As we have seen, voting is not the only form of political participation. It is, however, the most important one. Participation is important; yet voting is ultimately the litmus test of democracy. Democracy is impossible without free elections! Participation is not the main indicator of how democratic a regime is. Indeed, many authoritarian states have actively encouraged participation (e.g. in workers' councils in Yugoslavia under Tito (Pateman 1970, 87)). Elections are at the centre of democratic activity. We cherish that our system allows ordinary people to participate, and yet turnout-rates seem to show a downward trend. Why? Some argue that it is simply irrational to vote (see box 6.1).

The traditional belief was that lack of education, and membership of one of the lower classes explained low participation (there is still some evidence for this, as we have seen in chapter 3). Yet, the working classes are shrinking and the levels of education are rising. It is this failure of the pure sociological theories that have led political scientists to develop alternative models.

In the wake of the Second World War, the emergent science of politics sought to develop models and theories of electoral choice. One of the reasons for this was the failure of the opinion polls to predict the result of the US presidential election. Gallup and other polling firms had predicted in 1948 that the Republican Dewey would beat the incumbent Democrat Truman. Surprisingly – to them – Truman prevailed in the election. Why? Because the polling firms had phoned the respondents and (as it turned out) only the more wealthy citizens had a phone. As the more wealthy citizens were more likely to vote Republican, the result was that the opinion polls got it wrong. This would seem like a basic mistake, yet some might argue that the same mistake – albeit with different technology – is being made today.

When firms such as the British YouGov conduct opinion polls via the internet they arguably fail to take into consideration that a disproportionately high number of internet users are white middle-class males.

Box 6.1 *The paradox of voting*

Some theoreticians – of a *rational-choice* persuasion – think it a paradox that citizens bother to vote at all when the personal gain is so small, and the chance that their vote will be decisive is minimal. Have you ever wondered why people bother to vote, when the chance that they will cast the decisive vote is so minimal? Anthony Downs devoted a book to the subject. In *An Economic Theory of Democracy* (1957), Downs concluded that it was economically irrational to vote. The argument is as follows. Suppose there are two parties contesting an election. One party proposes a tax increase of 1 per cent. The other party does not advocate a tax increase. You favour the latter. However you are only one of several million voters. Your failure to cast your vote is unlikely to decide the outcome of the election. Moreover, finding the polling station is a bit of a hassle. So, given the minimal amount you can earn – and the cost of acquiring information – it is surprising that people bother to vote at all when there is a chance of only one in 28 million that you will cast the decisive vote. Yet many – indeed a majority – of the citizens do vote. Some would argue that people vote because they feel that it is their civic duty to do so. So is it a paradox that people vote? Proponents of so-called rational-choice theory believe the answer to be that voting is irrational. Political scientists of a more qualitative and historical persuasion tend to disagree (Blais 2000).

Party identification

There is an abundance of competing theories explaining low levels of participation. Declining participation is down to political factors, not social ones (Butler and Stokes 1974). Turnout goes up and down, and depends on the voters' involvement (or otherwise) with the campaign. Central to this theory is the notion of *party identification*: some voters are socialised to identify with one of the two major political parties, while others are not. Citizens who identify with a party (*party identifiers*) will tend to vote in every election and to vote for *their* party. Non-party identifiers, by contrast, will tend not to vote (unless prompted by short-term factors). The Michigan School – which is credited with the invention of this model – distinguished between three kinds of elections: maintaining elections; deviating elections; and realigning elections (Norris 1997, 78).

In a *maintaining* election the outcome will be decided by party-identifiers. Thus the party with the highest number of party identifiers will tend to win.

Not so in a *deviating* election, in which the non-identifiers will be prompted to turn out to vote (thus increasing turnout) for the minority party. In a deviating election the result differs from the 'normal vote', typically to the benefit of the party with the smallest number of party identifiers.

The model was originally developed for US presidential elections. Since the beginning of the 1930s a majority of Americans had identified themselves as 'Democrats'. In 1948 – when the Democrat Henry S. Truman won the election – the turnout was low and there were few if any issues that captured the voters. The result, consequently, reflected the 'normal' vote. The people who voted were the party identifiers and the Democrats won as they had more of them than the 'Republicans' did. The 1948 election was a typical *maintaining election*.

In 1956, when the Republican Dwight Eisenhower was re-elected, the turnout was impressive and the campaign was rich in short-term factors (e.g. the Soviet Union's invasion of Hungary and the Suez crisis). Many non-identifiers turned out to vote, and some Democrats defected to the Republicans (they returned two years later in the mid-term elections – when the turnout was low!). The 1956 presidential election was a *deviating election*.

Of course there are elections which altogether alter the identification of the voters. This typically happens during a national crisis. The presidential election in 1932 is an example of a *realigning* election. The Republicans had been the dominant party since the 1880s, and the majority of the voters were Republican party identifiers. (The election of Woodrow Wilson in 1912 was a *deviating election*. As expected, it followed the usual pattern of a high turnout and many short-term factors! In 1932 the Democrats succeeded in altering the electorate's party preferences for the following generations.)

Is this model valid in the UK? The answer depends on the distribution of partisan alignments. One would have expected that the Conservatives would be the political party with the highest number of party identifiers. The party, after all, governed the UK for more than two-thirds of the twentieth century. This dominance is not reflected in the distribution of party identifiers. The Labour Party had the largest number of party identifiers until 1979, when the Conservatives overtook that position in what we might describe as a re-aligning election. Focusing on the years prior to 1979, we would expect that the turnout would have been lowest in those years when the Labour Party won, as only committed voters are likely to turn out. In fact, it was not. Turnout was higher than the average (75.3 per cent) in the general elections which Labour won. We would have expected turnout to surge in 1970 (when the Tories won). It did not. Turnout dropped to 72.2 per cent.

Yet, while the model does not seem to explain the outcome or the turnout level in all the British elections since 1945 it is perhaps

Table 6.1 British general elections, 1945–2005

Year	Turnout (%)	Labour PI[a] (%)	Tory PI (%)	Winning party
1964	77.1	42	39	Labour
1966	75.8	45	36	Labour
1970	72.2	43	40	Conservative
1974	78.7	40	35	Labour
1974	72.8	40	34	Labour
1979	76.0	36	38	Conservative
1983	72.7	31	36	Conservative
1987	75.3	30	37	Conservative
1992	77.7	31	42	Conservative
1997	71.6	40	31	Labour
2001	59.9	40	28	Labour
2005	61.0	38	32	Labour

Note: [a] PI = party identifiers.
Source: *British Election Study* 1948–2005.

noteworthy that the elections in 1997, 2001 and 2005 are in conformance with the theory. The Labour Party won all three elections, had the highest number of party identifiers – and the turnout was low. It might be argued that these elections were quintessentially *maintaining elections*.

The 'science' of elections is called *psephology* (though the term is rarely used outside Britain). The word derives from the Greek word for pebble, namely *psefos*: the Greeks used small pieces of pebble for ballot paper, hence the name (Bogdanor 1991,503).

Today most psephologists believe that the Michigan model is past its sell-by date. The typology not only fails to explain the turnout-rate but it is also structurally undermined by the fact that the number of party identifiers is declining – a phenomenon often described as 'dealignment' (Sanders, Clarke, Stewart and Whiteley 2005).

This means that the usefulness of the concept as an *independent variable* has declined. But what else can account for this? Could it be, perhaps, that the system itself is to blame?

Participation and institutional factors

Some critics have argued that participation in the UK has dropped from 1990 and onwards due to an electoral system which is unfair and a disincentive to participating (McAllister 2001). British (and US) citizens are comparatively just as active as their German and French counterparts, yet the turnout in British (and in US) elections is now considerably below that of the two continental countries.

This was always the case in the USA, but not in Britain. While the turnout in Britain used to be above that of both countries, it is now barely above the 60 per cent mark. Why?

Critics of the current system say that the first-past-the-post electoral system (in which one candidate is elected in each constituency) creates a disincentive for a Labour voter living in a Tory constituency. There is little point in turning out to vote if one's vote is wasted on a candidate whose chances of winning the election are slim. Of course the symbolic importance of the very act of voting should never be discounted or underestimated. Some voters may see it as a manifestation of their personal beliefs that they vote for a candidate of a party with which they identify. Whether the candidate wins is not the only thing that matters. Having heroically sought to counter a trend – or having stayed true to the party supported by one's peers – may be *symbolically* important, yet

Table 6.2 Turnout rates in Western democracies, 1950–2000

Country	Electoral system	Turnout rate (%)
Austria	LPR[a]	84
Canada	FPP[b]	69
Denmark	LPR	83
Finland	LPR	72
France	SB[c]	69
Germany	MM[d]	77
Greece	LPR	80
Iceland	LPR	88
Irish Republic	STV[e]	66
Netherlands	LPR	78
New Zealand	MMS	80
Norway	LPR	76
Portugal	LPR	68
Spain	LPR	76
Sweden	LPR	87
Switzerland	LPR	46
Great Britain	FPP	78
United States	FPP	53

Notes: [a] list proportional representation; [b] first past the post; [c] mixed member; [d] second ballot; [e] single transferable vote (see box 6.2 on pp. 89. for explanations of electoral systems). Countries with compulsory voting (e.g. Australia, Belgium, Luxembourg and Italy) are not included.
Source: Dalton 1998.

it is unlikely that large numbers of voters attach much value to the act of voting. It is intuitively more likely that citizens will decide not to vote if their candidate has no chance of winning.

It is noteworthy that turnout in countries with PR is higher than in countries with the FPP electoral system (Blais and Carty 1990); yet there is no neat relationship. Switzerland (a country with LPR) has the lowest turnout rate in the Western World, though this is possibly because the very frequent referendums in that country has drained the voters' civic reserves, resulting in a comparatively low turnout (Qvortrup 2005, 35). (In party list PR, as in PR in general, seats are awarded in proportion to votes, i.e. a seat is awarded for each $1/N$ of the vote, in an N-seat election. But there are different ways of dealing with fractions, different 'allocation formulae'. It is beyond the scope of this discussion to give a detailed account of each. Suffice it to say that the most commonly known formulae are the Sainte-Laguë – used in Denmark, Norway and Sweden – and d'Hondt methods – used in Spain, Israel and Finland.)

In any case, the turnout rate in the Irish Republic is among the lowest, in spite of the proportionality of the MM electoral system used there. The turnout in Britain may have dropped, yet the average turnout is, in fact, one of the highest in the advanced industrial world! Institutional factors alone cannot explain turnout; we need historical and social factors as well. It is next to impossible to develop a general theory of turnout. Countries differ – and interest in politics varies from polity to polity.

Dissent and protest parties

Elections do not just function as a means of selecting the political elite as some have assumed (Schumpeter 1951); elections also have a 'signal effect'. Many choose to support a political party in order that this party will form a government that will enact and implement desired policies. However, these *instrumentalist* voters are not alone. Other voters – while not oblivious to instrumentalist concerns – may decide to show their dissent to the political system and the political debate by voting for fringe, protest and single-issue parties. Some may decide to vote for the 'Natural Law Party' (which advocates yoga and transcendental meditation to solve the country's problems). This is not, necessarily, because they believe, hope or expect that this party will form a government, but because– by voting for this party – they register dissent with a political system that focuses exclusively on material issues. The same logic may explain why some support the Monster Raving Loony Party, the British

National Party, the UK Independence Party, the Referendum Party or any single-issue candidates.

A vote for one of these parties or an individual candidate, like ex-BBC journalist Martin Bell (who was elected in 1997 on an anti-sleaze platform), can send a strong signal to the major parties that some issues are not being addressed satisfactorily – and might be an impetus for change.

A vote is not just a means of getting an individual elected; it is also a signifier, a message to those in power that all is not well and that the political options currently on offer are not satisfactory. Without opening up a whole new dimension of political research, it is important not to underestimate this *semiotic* side of electoral politics (Barthes 2000, 113). An example of this was provided by the Referendum Party.

In 1997 Sir James Goldsmith, a millionaire businessman, formed the Referendum Party with the sole aim of ensuring that a referendum was held before a future government would join the single European currency (the Euro). The party, which had no other policies than this, was comprised of individuals from the Right as well as from the Left (one of the latter being the environmentalist campaigner David Bellamy).

While Sir James's party did *not* succeed in getting any MPs elected, its aim was accomplished: Labour and the Conservatives adopted the referendum policy, and included manifesto pledges to the effect that a referendum would be held in the event of a decision to join the Euro (Qvortrup 2005, 116).

The success of the UK Independence Party (UKIP) in the European Parliamentary election in 2004 is another example of *protest-voting* which influenced a major party, in this instance the Conservative Party. Following the UKIP's success in the 1997, the new Conservative leader William Hague had adopted a much more critical approach to the European Union than his predecessor John Major had done. In 2004, UKIP sought to outdo the Conservatives once more by urging that the UK leave the EU altogether – a policy that Hague's successor as Conservative leader, Michael Howard, could not match for fear of being attacked by the Labour Party.

The result was that UKIP won the third highest number of votes –15.6 percent – and beat the Europhile Liberal Democrats, who secured only 14.4 Percent (Electoral Commission 2004). This success was arguably secured through the involvement of one-time Labour MP and TV chat-show host Robert Kilroy-Silk, who raised the party's profile in the media. The success of UKIP in the election – and the fact that the Conservatives out-polled Labour by 25.9 to 21.9 per cent – suggests that the LPR system has had the effect of allowing the voters express their preferences on policy issues, and has provided the sceptical UK voter with an opportunity to express his or her views on the European Union.

Box 6.2 *Electoral systems*

There are generally three 'families' of electoral systems:

* *majoritarian* systems: FPP, SB and the alternative vote (AV);
* *mixed* systems: MM; and
* *proportional* systems: STV, LPR.

The UK stands out as a country that uses almost all of those systems – the exception being the SB. STV is used in Northern Ireland; MM for elections to the Scottish Parliament and to the assemblies in London and Wales; AV for the London mayoral election; FPP for elections to the House of Commons; and LPR – the most widely used system on the Continent – for elections to the European Parliament.

AV   Voters indicate their preferences – first, second, third, etc., among the candidates. If a candidate receives an outright majority of first preferences, she is elected. If there is no such majority, the candidate with the lowest number of first preferences is dropped, and those preferences are downgraded to second preferences. This procedure is repeated until a majority winner is found. The system is used for the mayor of London elections.

FPP   The candidate with the highest number of votes in each constituency is elected.

LPR   Several candidates are elected in multi-member constituencies. Votes are entered for parties on *regional* lists (as in Denmark) or on a *whole-country* list (Israel and the Netherlands). The proportionality of a given LPR system depends on the number of seats per constituency: the higher the number, the higher the degree of proportionality.

MM   Each voter has two votes: one vote for a constituency MP (who is elected in an FPP system); the other from a list of additional members. In Britain the system is used for elections to the London and Welsh Assemblies and to the Scottish Parliament; the MM system is used also in Hungary, Germany and New Zealand).

SB   The SB system is the same as FPP, except the election is staged in two rounds. In the first round all candidates stand; the second round is a run-off between the candidates with the highest number of votes in the first. (This is utilised in France, but not currently in the UK.)

STV   Seats are allocated in multi-member constituencies. Voters rank candidates in order of preference. Seats are allocated at various stages of counting, and votes are redistributed according to preferences. (The system is used for the elections to the Northern Ireland Assembly, in the Republic of Ireland, for local elections in Scotland and for senate elections in Australia.)

Source: Nohlen *et al.* 2000.

Recent theories of electoral choice: class voting

'Class is the basis of political British party politics. All else is embellishment and detail' wrote Peter Pulzer (1967, 98). Today not all political scientists and sociologists would agree (see below). Some have declared class to be an obsolete concept, while others have made a case for a revision of the way that 'class' is defined and measured.

Class is a common enough concept, yet agreeing on a definition of 'class' is easier said than done. Karl Marx and Friedrich Engels (who were the first to use the concept in a way that is recognisable today) believed that 'society as a whole is more and more splitting up into two great hostile camps, into two great classes facing each other' (1985, 80). This view no longer accurately describes Western societies, but *class* is still an important concept.

Sociologists specialising in social stratification –whether Marxists or not – believe that society is considerably more complex than Marx and Engels tended to think. While there is an abundance of systems for social stratification and class-membership, most sociologists and political scientists focus on six categories of occupations:

- (A) *higher professional, managerial and administrative*, e.g. barristers, physicians, company directors, senior civil servants;
- (B) *intermediate professional, managerial and administrative*, university lecturers, teachers, junior executives;
- (C1) *supervisor, clerical and other non-manual*, e.g. secretaries, bank-tellers, police sergeants;
- (C2) *skilled manual*, e.g. electricians, machinists;
- (D) *semi-skilled and unskilled manual*, e.g. factory fitters, bus conductors;
- (E) *residual, casual workers, people on state benefits*, e.g. part-time and hospitality sector workers, the unemployed and pensioners.

While this categorisation would indicate that the dichotomous model of class antagonism is overly simplistic, some have sought to divide the six categories into two. The first three categories (A, B, and C1) can be described as the middle classes, while (C2–E) may be said to comprise the working classes. Based on this categorisation, political scientists have sought to determine whether class remains a predictor for voting behaviour.

Some influential sociologists have argued that class has ceased to be an important variable. American sociologist Ronald Inglehart, to mention but one, finds that 'the shift towards post-modern values has brought . . . a shift from political cleavages based on social class conflict towards cleavages based on cultural issues and quality of life concerns' (1997, 237). But has class ceased to be a reliable predictor of electoral choice?

Robert Alford, another American sociologist, has sought to develop a measure of the importance of 'class voting' (Alford 1967). The measure is statistically simple: the *Alford index of class voting* is found by subtracting the Labour Party's percentage share of the vote among non-manual workers (A–C1) from manual workers (C2–E). Thus if 20 percent of the middle-class voters vote for Labour, and 80 per cent of the working classes vote for this party, the Alford index of class voting will be 80 minus 20: 60.

Figures from the post-war era have consistently shown that the Alford index has shrunk – albeit the fall has been uneven. The Alford index was close to 50 in the 1940s – it is presently steady at around 10. This fall is the result, in part, of the Tories' increased success among C2 voters (often referred to, in the singular, as 'Essex man') and, in part, of an increasing propensity among professionals and the middle classes to vote Labour (especially after 1997). These figures – if read in isolation – would indicate the emergence of 'catch all parties', and the decline of class-based voting. The political parties no longer seek the support of distinct groups in society, as in the past. They seek rather to win support from all segments in society. The Labour Party is no longer the party of the working classes, but one that seeks also to attract middle-class voters.

One of the most thorough analyses of this phenomenon was carried out by Russell Dalton (2002). By applying the Alford index of class voting, Dalton found that class-based voting had declined considerably in the US, UK, Germany and France. He attributed this trend to changing economic and social conditions. Dalton argues that denominational voting also has declined in these four countries, the reasons for which could be found in technological and communications changes, as well as in the failure of parties to adequately handle contemporary political issues.

There is something intuitively convincing about this argument. British society has changed – and class structures have changed with it. The world of the 1950s was one of steel-mills, coal mines and manufacturing industry. Britain at the turn of the century is a country that bears all the hallmarks of post-industrial society: streets crowded with building societies, fast-food chains and an increasing proportion of the population working in the service sector. In 1971 roughly half of all males were working in the manufacturing industry; by the turn of the century this figure had dropped to one-third (see ONS 1995, 68).

By the mid-1980s it was widely believed that working-class voting had all but ceased to be a valuable predictor of citizens' voting behaviour. Yet, not everyone agreed. While no one sought to resurrect the 'orthodox' model (which suggested that economic class determines the way citizens vote), some political sociologists made a case for what has become known as the 'revision theory' of class voting.

Heath, Jowell and Curtice (1985) argued that there had been no class de-alignment. While they conceded that class sizes had changed since the early 1960s, they claimed that the *relative* class voting had not. The same proportion of workers continued to vote for the Labour Party, but the size of this group had shrunk. Hence the appearance of declining class voting.

There has been considerable debate about this revision theory. While the traditional – or Marxian – model of class antagonism appears of limited analytical value, the research seems to suggest that the rumours of the demise of class voting are exaggerated. One's position is society is still a predictor of one's political attitudes and behaviour. However, it is no longer the case that society is split into two antagonised camps.

Class voting and the Michigan model may – their differences notwithstanding – be described as *structural theories*. It is assumed that *structures*, such as socialisation, class and occupation, determine (or at least influence) the citizen's political attitudes and electoral behaviour. There need not be anything automatic in this. Class may be an important predictor of electoral behaviour because voters find it rational to vote for a political party that fights for their interests. The workers at the beginning of the twentieth century undoubtedly supported the Labour Party, and did so for economic reasons: Labour would increase the wages of the voters – the Tories would not.

Yet, class voting and the Michigan model are – as a general rule – based on the premiss that voters do not base their political behaviour on rational considerations, let alone on political issues. It is precisely these latter notions that lie at the heart of the alternative theories of electoral and political behaviour: the *issue voting* and *rational choice* theories. As was the case with the Michigan model, the inspiration for the alternative – or rival – theories were imported from America.

The Michigan model had painted a rather bleak picture of the voter as a socialised individual who – seemingly without reflection – voted for a political party out of psychological attachment. This model – while inconsistent with the basic premiss of democratic theory – was supported by survey evidence in the 1940s and 1950s. The picture seemingly changed in the 1960s – not least in the USA. Growing discontent, the student revolt, increased political awareness in the wake of the civil rights movement and the Vietnam war led to a revision of the traditional models.

In *The Changing American Voter* (2002) Verba, Nie and Petrocik found evidence of a considerable political sophistication, one that was – albeit with a slightly different focus – shared by proponents of so-called 'economic' voting. The theory of economic voting, like that of 'issue voting', was inspired by US research. In the *Responsible Electorate*, published in 1966, Texan political scientist, V.O. Key advanced, what he called the 'perverse and unorthodox theory that voters are not fools, they appraise past performances and past actions' (Key 1966, 7).

Key's study was not clad in sophisticated statistical models, which has subsequently become the hallmark of the approach (Lewis-Beck and Rice 1990). Key's significance lay in instituting a paradigm based on 'retrospective voting'. Yet, unlike Key, most of his followers have based their models on economic issues. Voters, it is argued, consider a government's macro-economic record and base their electoral choice on their evaluation of its performance.

The theory of economic voting is an American invention which, in recent years, has spread from its native soil to other democracies. One of the most impressive examples of the model's ability to predict elections is provided by British political scientist David Sander's correct prediction that the Conservative Party would win the 1992 UK general election (which the opinion polls had all but handed to the Labour Party (Sanders 1991).

By using what was called the 'feel-good factor' – a measure of the voters' confidence in their own economic fortunes – Sanders could predict the outcome of the election. Moreover, the model could also explain the Tories' defeat in 1997. Whether this model yields anything more than a lucky guess remains to be seen. Some would perhaps argue that the model fails to explain the underlying reasons for electoral behaviour. Yet it should not be seen in isolation: the various models of electoral behaviour complement each other – they are not necessarily alternatives.

Citizens and the mass media

'The people is never corrupted, but is often deceived, and on such occasions only does it seem to will what is bad' (Rousseau 1964, 23). The Swiss philosopher's assessment of the citizens' propensity to be lured into voting for politicians and policies (to which they in reality were opposed) seems to resonate with many people's recent view of the power of the press – not least the press itself.

The election in 1997 is a pertinent example of this. The Labour Party and Tony Blair himself was at pains to win the support of the *Sun* newspaper. Perhaps understandably, the party wanted to prevent a repetition of the 1992 general election in which, it was believed, the *Sun* had helped the Tories to a fourth consecutive victory. Following a personalised campaign against Mr Kinnock (then Labour leader), the paper took credit for the Labour Party's defeat with the front-page headline 'It was the *Sun* wot won it'.

Anxious to prevent another Tory victory, Kinnock's successor Tony Blair pulled out all the stops to ensure the support of the *Sun*. He actively courted the proprietor Rupert Murdoch, and succeeded in shifting the paper into the Labour camp. Psephologists are not entirely convinced that the *Sun*'s role was crucial. Although Labour secured the paper's support, the party did not gain any votes after the *Sun*'s decision to back Blair. It is a conspicuous fact that John Major's embattled Government won the campaign in 1997 (improved its standing in the opinion polls) – but not the election. The hugely unpopular party did not suffer the catastrophic defeat that the opinion polls had predicted. There was, newspaper endorsements notwithstanding, a bedrock beneath which the popularity of the Tories did not sink.

This fact seems to indicate that the Labour Party gained little from winning over Mr Murdoch to its side. Yet, it is possible that the support worked in more subtle ways. It is always tempting to extrapolate from the big picture to individual behaviour. While the net-result may have seemed meagre – indeed non-existent – it is possible that Labour influenced *Sun* readers, while failing to hold on to erstwhile supporters reading other newspapers, e.g. the *Daily Mirror*. In the terminology of political consultants, Labour 'failed to solidify its base'.

To determine the effect on the Labour Party's fortunes in 1997 of the *Sun*'s support requires a micro-analysis of individual voters' attitudes and voting decisions. What we are particularly interested in is whether the readers of the *Sun* newspaper were more prone to switch to the Labour Party during the campaign and, indeed, whether the readers of the papers that remained faithful to the Tory Party (the *Daily Mail*, the *Daily Telegraph* and the *Express*) stayed loyal to the party, or whether they jumped on the Labour bandwagon. We can get an indication of this from table below.

Table 6.3 shows the probability that voters changed their allegiance after having read one of the newspapers which advocated support for a particular political party. Take a *Sun*-reading voter who, a year before the election, had said that he would vote for the Conservative Party. Following the *Sun*'s decision to back Labour the likelihood of this voter supporting the Tories dropped by 6 per cent!

Table 6.3 Newspaper-reading and change in party support over the 1997
          electoral campaign

Paper read regularly	Change Con	Change Lab	Change Lib Dem
Tory faithful papers[a]	+1	−4	+5
The *Sun*	−6	+1	+0
Labour faithful papers[b]	+1	−11	+3

Notes: [a] *Daily Express, Daily Mail, Telegraph, The Times*; [b] *Daily Mirror,*
  Guardian.
Source: *British Election Study* 1997.

The figure seems to indicate that the Conservative Party increased its support from the readers of the Tory papers, whereas the Labour Party was unable to make net gains among these voters. The figures also indicate that the *Sun* improved the Labour Party's fortunes.

The Conservatives had lost support from the *Sun*'s readers (–6), whereas the Labour Party seems to have gained – albeit not much (+ 1). However, this gain was offset by the considerable drop in support from voters reading the Labour faithful papers. Compared to the year preceding the election the Labour Party dropped 11 points among the readers of the papers that had supported Blair all along. The *Sun* was not 'wot won it' in 1997 – in fact one might speculate that the Labour Party would not have lost quite so many of supporters had they not courted the Conservative press.

While Table 6.3 indicates that the *Sun* modestly improved Labour's standing, the figure does not provide any explanation for why the Liberal Democrats were able to improve their standing among all groups – except among *Sun* readers. No paper supported the Liberal Democrats (though the *Independent* and the *Observer* urged their readers to vote tactically, i.e. that a Liberal voter should vote for, say, a Labour candidate if the Liberal candidate did not have a chance of beating the Tory candidate, and vice versa). Can we explain this model theoretically?

Opinion leaders: the two-step hypothesis

A classic model of the media's influence on citizens – especially in elections – is the so-called 'opinion leaders' model' – also known as the two-step hypothesis. Developed by Paul Lazarsfelt and his colleagues in the 1950s, the model sought to explain the 1948 presidential election in the USA.

The authors claim that voters are not *directly* influenced by the media or advertising, but that the effect is *indirect* (Lazarsfeld, Berelson and Gaudet 1988). When making decisions, most people rely on what Lazersfeld called an 'opinion leader'.

The opinion leader is an individual in what sociologists call a 'primary group' whose views are trusted on a subject. A primary group is a small group characterised by 'face-to-face' interaction (e.g. a family or a social group). By contrast 'secondary groups' are larger groups such as a trade union or a political party.

Every primary group will be characterised by a division of labour. In making their decisions, the members of a primary group will tend to listen to an opinion leader, someone in the primary group whom others listen to in matters concerning politics.

The media will – according to this model – only change the opinions of the voters at large, if they manage to persuade the opinion leaders. The process goes as follows:

Mass media → opinion leaders → citizens

Interestingly, opinion leaders can be found across all ages and levels of social status (high, middle and low), though often women turn for advice to other women within the same social status, as opposed to seeking out those of higher social status. Katz and Lazarsfeld – in a later study – also concluded that opinion leaders were concentrated among the wives and mothers in large families. This group tended to have more experience and involvement with daily marketing issues (Lazarsfeld and Katz 1955, 19).

Finally, the researchers determined that 'highly gregarious women (those who have a large number of friends and belong to several organizations) are more likely to be opinion leaders' (ibid.). Lazarsfeld and Katz were not oblivious to the implications of the model for democratic theory:

> What we shall call opinion leadership, if we may call it leadership at all, is leadership at its simplest: it is casually exercised, sometimes unwitting and unbeknown, within the smallest grouping of friends, family members, and neighbours. It is not leadership on the high level of a Churchill, or of a local politico, nor even social elite. It is at quite the opposite extreme: it is the almost invisible, certainly inconspicuous, form of leadership at the person-to-person level of ordinary, intimate, informal, everyday contact. (Ibid., 138)

Although this model was developed many years ago, it is still influential among sociologists – and among marketing people, who actively seek to utilise the results of this research! (Black 1982). Whether this model explains the behaviour of voters in Britain – or indeed elsewhere – is contested on empirical grounds. But it does provide a model for thinking about the media's influence which challenges the crude models of the mass media's unmediated influence over the voters.

Summing up

What determines the way people vote? Why do some vote for the Tories while others vote for the Labour Party? The answer traditionally has been *class*. Today the answer is less clear-cut, for class is no longer what it used to be – society is no longer split into two antagonistic classes facing one another, as Marx and Engels claimed. But neither has class ceased altogether to be a predictor of how individuals will cast their ballots. Citizens from the lower echelons of society continue to support the Labour Party in greater numbers than they support the Conservative Party. Yet voting is no longer determined by class – and it is questionable if it ever was.

Another answer is *psychological attachment*. In the decades after the Second World War it was popular to see electoral behaviour and outcomes as results of the voters' identification with the different parties.

Scholars like Angus Campbell and his colleagues at the University of Michigan predicted that in elections with low turnout the parties with the highest number of *identifiers* would win. Only when the minority party managed to capture the agenda – as the Republicans did in 1952 and 1956 – would there be a change in government. They called the former a *maintaining* and the latter a *deviating* election. This model was related in part to the class model: the voters' attachment to the political parties was in large measure the product of socialisation (with working-class voters more likely to vote for the party of the Left). Yet the Michigan model's predictive powers began to wane as a declining number of voters considered themselves as party identifiers. Factors other than class and social allegiance were taking on greater importance.

Issues are increasingly important in politics, not least economic issues. While economic conditions cannot explain the outcome of elections, it is nevertheless noteworthy that some analysts have had considerable success predicting outcomes by using economic figures.

Does this trend supersede traditional explanations, such as the role of the press? The importance of the press in influencing voters' behaviour has always been disputed. No consensus has emerged, however, and many scholars (perhaps even a majority) claim that the primary role of the press is its agenda-setting function. Unable to tell voters what to think, the major newspapers are stunningly successful in telling voters what to think about. While the press does not decide elections, it has occasionally happened that a paper's support of a particular party has succeeded in changing the voting intentions of some of its readers. There are some indications that this happened in 1997 when the *Sun* switched allegiance from the Tories to the Labour Party. However, the increase in the popularity of the Liberal Democrats – a party that received no backing from any of the newspapers – obviously shows the limits to that model.

In this chapter we have looked at elections and electoral systems, considering various electoral systems, which can be divided into three families:

- *majoritarian* (AV, FPP, and SB);
- *proportional* (STV, LPR); and
- *mixed systems* (MM).

Different explanations of why citizens make electoral choices have been examined; the Michigan school, models of class voting and retrospective voting. We considered also the emergence of new concepts, such as 'de-alignment'.

Voting is not always just an instrumental act, aimed at selecting representatives for parliaments, city councils and assemblies. Occasionally voters may use their vote to protest by opting for such parties as the British Nationalist Party. This is not necessarily a sign of support for those parties' views, but is rather a way of communicating dissent and discontent with the traditional parties. We know a great deal about elections – and about why people cast their votes – but new questions continue to emerge, which is partly why studying elections and voting is so fascinating.

It might be instructive at this point to consider – in some detail – the result of people's engagement in politics. Citizen democracy has often been criticised for assuming that people have access to unlimited information. Moreover, it is often argued that citizens' influence should be limited as MPs have the time and expertise to consider matters more thoroughly (Ortega y Gasset 1937; Schumpeter 1951). To sustain this view it is necessary to consider what Parliament does and what powers it possesses vis-à-vis the Executive. We will see that the UK Parliament's powers are in some respects negligible.

7

Excursus: the power of the representatives

We have seen that citizens are involved in government both as instigators of action and when they are called on to make decisions. Yet, while a strong case can be made for using elements of direct democracy as a complement to popular government, there have always been those who more or less fundamentally reject citizen involvement in anything but elections – as Schumpeter did (see chapter 2).

One of the arguments against citizen politics is that it is impossible for the whole body of the nation to deliberate on matters of public importance. This view is at the core of the theory of representative government and was perhaps most famously summed up by Edmund Burke in his speech to the electors of Bristol in 1774 when he stated: 'Parliament is a deliberative assembly of one nation, with one interest, that of the whole; where, not local purposes, not local prejudices ought to guide, but the general good, resulting from the general reason as a whole' (1902, 447). But is this an accurate description. Does Parliament *deliberate*? And is it correct that MPs are those best placed to make rational and considered judgements and decisions?

While it is common to criticise the ordinary voters for their alleged populism, and to reject use of the methods of direct democracy as voters allegedly are prone to make ill-considered decisions. It is important to note that the same critique rarely extends to legislatures. Politicians often reject the use of, say, referendums because the voters have enacted controversial legislation (e.g. the abolition of property taxes in the so-called 'Proposition 13' referendum in California in 1978). But few people reach the conclusion that representative democracy is undesirable if the representatives reach similarly controversial decisions. It is conveniently forgotten that 'the record of representative government is an imperfect one' (Cronin 1989, 91), as illustrated by, for instance, the decision in Tennessee in 1996 to sack teachers who taught evolution as 'fact' (*New York Times*, 29 February 1996). This, of course, is an American example. How, then, does Britain fare? Are

British parliamentarians more likely to have reached informed decisions and to hold government to account?

'The mother of all parliaments' was how the radical politician John Bright described the UK legislature in the Victorian age, a self-congratulatory narrative still widely used (Wright 2000, 195). While it is questionable if this description is historically accurate – the Icelandic *Althingi* from 930 CE is arguably older (Jones 2004, 200) – the Westminster Parliament has often been seen as the archetypal legislature, the epitome of a representative democracy in which the elected members of the people hold the executive to account (ibid).

I argue in this chapter that this view is neither empirically accurate nor theoretically justified. Indeed, more than any other legislative body, the UK Parliament is uniquely controlled by the government of the day. In the word of one observer it is a 'fact that in Britain the executive is particularly strong and parliament commensurably weak' (Wright 2004, 867).

However, we should ask whether this assessment applies following the spate of reforms breathtakingly undertaken by the Labour Government since 1997. From the time it came to power, the Government led by Tony Blair has presided over considerable constitutional changes: devolution to Scotland and Wales; the introduction of new electoral systems; the incorporation of the European Convention of Human Rights into British law; the reform of the House of Lords (see below) and the modernisation of the House of Commons. As a result of the latter, Parliament sits at different times, a second debating chamber (Westminster Hall) has been added, more bills are considered in draft, business is routinely programmed and select committees have acquired more resources and tasks. Does this mean that the British Parliament has fundamentally changed? Are the reforms different from similar reforms undertaken in the 1970s and 1980s under the stewardships of, respectively, Richard Crossman and St John Stevas?

While seemingly impressive, the changes have failed to limit executive dominance of the House of Commons. Indeed, a strong case could be made for the view that the recent reforms have in fact strengthened government's control over legislature.

As the workings of the UK's political institutions are the result of a long historical process, it is necessary to understand the evolution of the Westminster Parliament. According to Dahl, the beginnings of representative government were the

> assemblies summoned by monarchs, or sometimes the nobles themselves, to deal with important matters of state: revenues, wars, royal succession, and the like. In the typical pattern, those summoned were drawn from and

were intended to represent the various estates, with the representatives from each estate meeting separately. Over time, the estates diminished to two, lords and commoners, who were of course represented in separate houses. (1989, 29)

This is true for the British Parliament, which can trace its origins to the Anglo-Saxon *Witenagemot* established by William of Normandy in 1066. The Norman king sought the advice of a council of tenants-in-chief and church leaders to ensure the legitimacy of his rule following his successful invasion of Britain.

In 1215, this assembly secured from King John (Lackland) the right to block tax increases. Shortly thereafter, in 1265, Simon de Montfort, a nobleman who led a baronial revolt against Henry III, summoned the first elected Parliament (Jones 2004, 200). From a comparative historical perspective this assembly was surprisingly representative – although it fell well short of what we today would consider a democratic legislature! The franchise extended to all who owned the freehold of land to an annual rent of 40 shillings (so-called 'forty-shilling freeholders').

This institution gradually evolved into a bicameral legislature, established by Edward III, who separated Parliament into two Houses: one including the nobility and higher clergy (the House of Lords), the other including the knights and burgesses (the House of Commons). This system remained until the defeat of the Royalists (who wished to curb the powers of Parliament) in the English Civil War (1649).

The so-called 'interregnum' (1650–1660) was a period of considerable change in Britain's system of representative government. Oliver Cromwell abolished the House of Lords, and the power of the executive was – at least in theory – limited by Parliament. Yet, although Cromwell had fought for the rights of Parliament, he was by no means an egalitarian. Indeed, during his rule radical groups, such as the Levellers (see chapter 2), advocated, in the famous Putney Debates (1647), that voting rights should be extended to 'wage-earners and those in receipt of alms, and beggars' (McPherson 1962, 107).

This radicalism – while never implemented – led to a backlash. The bi-cameral system was re-established in 1660, following the death of Cromwell, and finally formalised into something resembling the present system during the Glorious Revolution in 1688.

During the eighteenth century Parliament was *not* a legislature in the sense that it made the laws! Yet power gradually began to shift from the sovereign. By the end of the reign (1660–1727) of George I, the ministers appointed by the King could only be removed with the explicit consent of Parliament (parliamentarianism). But Parliament in those days was mainly synonymous with the House of Lords – political influence tends to be synonymous with economic power! The principle of ministerial responsibility to the Lower House did not develop until the nineteenth century. In the previous century members of the House of Commons were elected via an antiquated electoral system under which constituencies of vastly different sizes existed. Thus, the borough of Old Sarum, with 7 voters, could elect 2 members, as could the borough of Dunwich, which had completely disappeared into the sea due to land erosion!

In many cases, members of the Upper House controlled tiny constituencies, known as 'pocket boroughs' or 'rotten boroughs', and could ensure the election of their relatives or supporters. Many seats in the House of Commons were 'owned' by the Lords. One famous beneficiary of this system was the philosopher Edmund Burke who, after he lost his seat in Bristol, was elected in the rotten borough of Malton, which was controlled by his patron Lord Rockingham (White 2002, 11).

After the reforms of the nineteenth century (beginning in 1832 and deepened in 1867), the electoral system in the Lower House was much more regularised. No longer dependent on the Upper House for their seats, members of the House of Commons began to grow more assertive. (This was in part because the economic power had shifted from the landed gentry to the class of wealthy entrepreneurs.)

It was largely on the basis of this system that the constitutional lawyer Albert Venn Dicey developed his doctrine of the sovereignty of Parliament, according to which 'Parliament has the right to make or unmake any law whatever' (Dicey 1982, xxxvi). However, Dicey did not – though he is commonly misunderstood to have done – argue that the elected chamber was the supreme power under the British Constitution. Indeed, he was adamant that 'Parliament consists of the King, the House of Lords, and the House of Commons acting together' (ibid.).

While Dicey's doctrine became dominant in legal circles, the most accurate account, politically, of the British Constitution was developed by Walter Bagehot, a journalist and one-time editor of the *Economist*, who in *The English Constitution* of 1867 – a little prematurely – had categorised the Lords as belonging to the *dignified* – as distinct from the *efficient* part of the Constitution. In his view, the British political system had changed from being one dominated by the aristocracy to one dominated by a government selected by the commoners.

The superior role of the Commons became a reality in 1910, when the Lords' powers were restricted to delaying for two years legislation passed by the Lower House (Emden 1962, 225). This strengthening of the Commons at the Lords' expense was taken one step further with the Parliament Act of 1949 which reduced the peers' delaying power to one year and gave the Commons the opportunity to exercise a suspensive veto. Finance bills – if certified as such by the Speaker of the House (Shell 1999, 199) – could be enacted within a month.

The most recent fundamental change came in 1999 when the Labour Government removed all but ninety-two of the hereditary peers in the Lords as a first stage of Lords' reform. However, it is still the case that hereditary peers wield influence over legislation by virtue of birth rather than by an elected or democratic mandate. This is internationally unique among democratic countries! The members of the House of Lords are appointed by the Prime Minister, though since May 2000 non-partisan members have been recommended by the House of Lords Appointments Commission (HLAP). In addition, there are 26 bishops and archbishops of the Church of England and 12 law lords. In no other democratic country has a similar anachronism been allowed to continue to exist!

What have these changes meant for the power relation between government and Parliament? John Stuart Mill once noted that 'the meaning of representative government is that the whole people, or some numerous portion of them, exercise through deputies, periodically elected by themselves, the ultimate controlling power' (Mill 1991, 269). It is questionable – in the strictest sense of the word – whether Britain has ever satisfied this criterion – though the period from 1832 to 1867 (during which Mill was an MP) did approximate this ideal.

Moreover, Mill's portrait of Parliament was more normative than descriptive. His contemporary Walter Bagehot's account is the more accurate – and remains so to this day. Bagehot wrote:

> The main function of the House of Commons is one which we know quite well, though common constitutional speech does not recognise it. The House of Commons is an electoral chamber; it is the assembly which chooses our president (Bagehot 2001, 99).

This modest role distinguishes the UK Parliament sharply from the US Congress, and even legislatures in mainland Europe. The US Congress and, to a degree, the German *Bundestag* and *Bundesrat*, are empowered to restrict the powers of government through checks and balances, and to propose and enact legislation.

The UK Parliament's position, by contrast, is much more modest. Bagehot listed five functions (ibid., 100):

- an *elective* function: to choose the government of the day;
- an *expressive* function: to give voice to the collective mind of the British people;

- a *teaching* function: to educate the public through competent debates and discussions;
- an *informing* function: to hold government to account, and;
- a *legislative* function: to approve or reject bills (typically proposed by government).

Parliament – at least to a certain degree – was able to carry out these functions in earlier times, though there is now a 'widespread recognition in the United Kingdom that there is an imbalance in the relationship between Parliament and government' (Norton 2000, 1).

While a whole literature has focused on the so-called 'decline of parliament thesis' (Beer 1966; Bryce 1921), there is little evidence to support the claim that Britain has had a strong legislature like that of the USA, or even a modestly strong one like Norway's (Rasch 2004). To use a distinction developed by US academic Nelson Polsby, the British Parliament is an 'arena' legislature, not a 'transformative' one like its American counterpart (Polsby 1990, 129).

To be sure, British MPs can introduce legislation, and occasionally this gets enacted (David Steele, a Liberal MP, got abortion legalised through a Private Member's Bill in the 1960s), but as a general rule – i.e. in more that 90 percent of the cases – legislation is introduced by the Government.

There are three procedures under which MPs may introduce legislation:

- the ballot
- the ten-minute rule, and
- ordinary presentation procedure.

In addition a bill initiated in the Lords may be taken up by a member of the House of Commons. However, as noted, these mechanisms are rarely used.

That the *raison d'être* of the UK Parliament is debate rather than legislation is evidenced by formal institutional structures, especially in the structure of committees. The US Congress is characterised by strong committees with long-term members (e.g. Senators Richard Lugar and Sam Nunn on the Defence Committee and the late Daniel Patrick Moynihan on the Finance Committee). Indeed, Woodrow Wilson once noted that 'Congressional government is committee government' (quoted in English 2003, 61). The reverse is the case in the UK, where the committees are weak.

The UK Parliament has two kinds of committees: *standing committees* and *select committees*. The former are ad hoc committees scrutinising proposed legislation (their membership is determined by the Whips' Office); select committees are slightly more powerful and are typically comprised of senior back-benchers. Yet there are exceptions.

While the Chief Whip is usually in control, the appointment of select committee chairs is not entirely within her gift, and even the Blair Government (with a majority of more than 160 MPs in 2001) had to bow to pressure and reinstate the independent-minded Gwyneth Dunwoody as chair of the Transport Committee, despite the wishes of the Chief Whip Hilary Armstrong. However this example is very much the exception that confirms the rule.

The establishment of select committees in 1979 strengthened Parliament, even though membership of the committee is not permanent and despite the fact that the committees have little staff and are unable to effectively challenge ministers with hundreds of advisors and civil servants in the Whitehall departments. It is, therefore, questionable whether these committees in reality have strengthened the House of Commons. Tam Dayell, a veteran MP (1964–2004), observed on his retirement:

> One of the great changes, which is widely applauded, is the development of the departmental select committee. For me, the jury is still out . . . What I concluded was that any MP who wanted to campaign on a subject within the provenance of a select committee would be well advised not to agree to membership of that committee. (2005, 380)

What exactly are the mechanisms which account for this relative weakness of the Westminster Parliament? One answer, proposed by Tony Wright – an MP and political scientist! – is that the 'textbook talk about Parliament's role in scrutiny and accountability frequently fails to get inside the skin of an institution whose members have a quite different agenda'. According to Dr Wright, the MPs 'want to be promoted at best and re-elected at worst' (Wright 2004, 85). It is important to bear this in mind when analysing Parliament.

Government and agenda-setting in the UK

Rasch (2004) distinguishes three means by which an executive can influence legislative outcomes:

- *institutional*: constitutional or parliamentary rules enable government to prevent – or severely limit – amendments to legislation (e.g. the ten-minute rule and the guillotine);
- *majoritarian*: by controlling a majority of seats in Parliament governments can impose their will (in Britain this is done through the Whips' Office), and;

- *positional*: by occupying the middle ground of the political spectrum, the governments can select the final outcomes of parliamentary debates even in the absence of institutional advantages or stable majorities.

While the latter option is far from unknown in the UK (governments in the 1950s in particular made use of positional advantages), it is the first two factors that are most frequently considered and debated in Britain. Aspects of institutional and majoritarian advantages are analysed in what follows.

Institutional advantages

The rediscovery of institutions, i.e. the acknowledgment that 'institutions matter' has had a profound impact in political science in recent years, both in rational-choice theory (Tsebelis 1994) and more generally in comparative politics (Weaver and Rockman 1993). Hot on the heels of this research, empirical work has shown that governments may have several institutional advantages *vis-à-vis* Parliament (Rasch 1995, 2004).

As noted elsewhere, Governments can assume a privileged position in any number of ways, e.g. through time constraints, closed or restrictive rules, expansive rules, sequencing rules, voting order rules, vote-counting and gate-keeping rules, and exclusive government jurisdiction (McKelvey 1976; Schofield 1978; Rasch 2004).

Not all of these apply in the UK, but for a country without a written constitution, British parliamentary procedure is bewilderingly rule driven. Two particular institutional devices are important, time constraints (including gate-keeping rules) and exclusive government jurisdiction. Time constraints are by far the most important of these- and will, therefore, be given a more extensive coverage.

TIME CONSTRAINTS AND THE COMMONS

Under normal circumstances a bill goes through five six stages (first reading, second reading, the committee stage, the report stage, third reading and the House of Lords stage), before it receives royal assent. As Parliamentary procedure is entirely controlled by the Leader of the House (a cabinet minister), who is responsible for the legislative time-table, Parliament is given limited time to depart from the established schedule.

While the first and the second readings are a formality, it is possible for a standing committee to amend legislation. However, this is a rarity, as the members of that committee are selected by the whips.

When legislation is amended it is typically at the report stage, as was the case when Tony Blair's Terrorism Bill was amended in November 2005. (The Government had proposed that terrorist suspects could be held for 90 days, but the Commons only accepted 28 days and moved an amendment to that effect.)

A government might find that its proposed legislation is challenged (typically) at the report stage (when the Bill is debated by the whole House). To fend off such a challenge, the Leader of the House can move a *time-table motion*. Prior to 1998, there were two ways in which the House of Commons could time-table bills:

- allocation of time (commonly called 'guillotine' motions – a rarely used practice dating back to 1887) to speed up or secure the passage of a bill, and to prevent the opposition from obstructing the bill, and;
- the 'usual channels' – voluntary, informal, unpublished and, ultimately, unenforceable agreements between government and opposition whips.

The guillotine has traditionally been government's most efficient means of curtailing a debate or of preventing the opposition from engaging in (perceived or real) obstructing tactics. Introduced in 1887 to end Irish MPs' attempts to filibuster the Criminal Law Amendment (Ireland) Bill, the main function of the guillotine is to set a time for the third reading of a bill. According to William Smith – a minister at the time – the device was necessary as Parliament had 'arrived at the fourth month of the session and we have practically done nothing except to consider the measure now before the House . . . the whole course of legislation has been stopped' (*House of Commons Debates*, 10 June 1887, col. 1596).

This might seem a sensible view, though it should not be forgotten that democracy is also about respecting minority views. It is worth bearing in mind that Erskine May's *Parliamentary Practice* (the standard reference work on procedure) finds that guillotine motions

> may be regarded as the extreme limit to which procedure goes in affirming the rights of the majority as the expense of the minorities of the House, and it cannot be denied that they are capable of being used in such a way as to upset the balance, generally so carefully preserved, between the claims of business and the rights of debate. (1997, 411)

Government has to a degree recognised the draconian nature of the guillotine, and has tended to restrict its use, though there have been periods when this curtailing measure has been used with rather more frequency. From a historical perspective it is, perhaps, interesting that there were fewer guillotine motions (14) in the period 1921–1945 than in 1945–1975 (30). We might have expected that government had less reason for curbing the debate in the hey-day of the two-party system as party unity would have limited the use of the device. Conversely, one might have expected a more widespread use of the guillotine at time when the 'effective number of parties' (Laakso and Taagapera 1979, 3) was higher in the Commons, as it was in the 1920s and the 1930s.

This line of reasoning misses the point. Certainly party unity is important, but it is largely irrelevant to the use of the guillotine, which is a mechanism to limit (perceived) obstruction by the opposition minority. The guillotine, consequently, is used chiefly during periods of ideological disagreement. In the aftermath of the Second World War, the Labour Government thus guillotined the debates on the nationalisation of iron and steel (1948) and on the establishment of the NHS (1951). The greater the ideological divide between government and opposition the greater use of the guillotine. There was little need to curtail the debates in the years of national unity governments in the 1930s, so that the mechanism was rarely used.

In recent years, the use of the guillotine has been limited, and there have been attempts at modernising the procedures. But it is questionable whether these efforts have changed the way Parliament works. As Tony Wright has put it:

> There has been much talk of 'modernising' Parliament since 1997, with a special parliamentary committee established for this purpose, but its fruits so far have been meagre. 'Modernisation' can anyway be a weasel word: it can mean procedural changes to enable the executive to process its business more tidily, or to hold it effectively to account. The former has so far been preferred to the latter. (2004, 91)

TIME CONSTRAINTS AND THE LORDS

'Never mind, the Lords will sort it out for us.' This reportedly is what a backbench MP told a colleague after the Commons had failed to soften the Blair Government's anti-terror legislation in 2001. And the Lords duly proceeded and sent the Bill back to the Commons (ibid., 92).

The House of Lords is more than merely a 'dignified' part of the Constitution, as Bagehot had asserted in the 1860s. In some ways – to borrow another phrase from the Victorian sage – it is in some ways a more 'efficient' part of the Constitution than their 659 colleagues in the Lower House. Despite its (to put it mildly!) dubious democratic legitimacy, the Upper House wields considerable power over the legislative process, as especially Labour governments have learned to their cost (Tsebelis and Money 1998).

The Lords have generally abided by the so-called Salisbury Convention, according to which the Upper House should not obstruct a bill proposed in the governing party's election manifesto (Shell 1999, 202). If the Lords still reject a bill, the Commons can *in extremis* invoke the Parliament Act 1949, although they have done so rarely. Since 1949 four Acts have been passed into law without the consent of the House of Lords, namely: the War Crimes Act 1991, the European Parliamentary Elections Act 1999, the Sexual Offences (Amendment) Act 2000, and the Hunting Act 2004. All but one of these was enacted by Labour – perhaps an indication of the Conservative bias in the Upper House. In other words, the Lords can still – the Parliament Act notwithstanding – upset a government's time-table; indeed they are able to exercise a *de facto* 'pocket veto', as bills introduced in one session may not be carried over into the next session.

The scope for such interventions has been reduced of late. Following a proposal from the Modernisation Committee in 1998 – but not implemented before 2002 – it has been agreed that in 'defined circumstances and subject to certain safeguards', government bills can be carried over from one session to the next. While seemingly modest, this reform has further reduced the powers of the Lords to block or delay legislation (Modernisation Committee, Third Report, 23).

While the Modernisation Committee officially was seeking to strengthen Parliament, there is little indication that this has happened (Peele 2004, 220). As one critical observer put it: 'Bills are discussed, on average, for 71/2 hours, but this allocation is not equally distributed between or within Acts. During the Commons processes, much legislation is therefore passed with little or no scrutiny' (Parlianet 2004).

EXCLUSIVE GOVERNMENT JURISDICTION

Most Acts of Parliament leave it to the executive to determine the finer points of regulation, through so-called *statutory instruments* – often abbreviated SI (Page 2001). One particularly contentious aspect of SIs is the use of 'Henry VIII Clauses', which enable a government to amend or repeal primary legislation. While a minister can be called to defend an SI in either of the two Chambers, there is little Parliament can do. In a report by the independent Hansard Society, it was argued that the use of SIs had become a threat to parliamentary scrutiny of legislation (Hansard 1992). Or, in the colourful phrase of MP Bob Cryer, the 'torrent of [statutory instruments] has turned Parliament into a sausage machine' (*House of Commons Debates*, 17 February 1993, Vol. 219, col. 319).

Whether this assessment is correct is, however, debatable – especially from a comparative perspective. Through the Joint Committee on

Statutory Instruments (JCSI), Parliament can examine SI, and indeed – in theory but *never* in practice – vote them down. While the 'opportunity to provide such scrutiny is guaranteed only in relatively few cases when the parent legislation requires it' (Page 2001, 157–58), this broadly negative conclusion does not, however, imply that Parliament is powerless and impotent rubber-stamp. As Page argued: 'Parliament has a crucial and pervasive impact on the technical, but not the policy, aspects of the delegated legislative process. Most lawyers try to draft regulations as if JCSI is looking over their shoulder' (ibid., 174).

Thus while the 'scrutiny role of Parliament appears at first sight to be rather weak . . . Parliament nevertheless offers significant opportunities for moving issues out of the obscure world of everyday politics and into a more familiar world of inter- and intra-party political conflict' (ibid., 175). Further, the fact that SI are debated at all in the UK is arguably a significant difference between our system and other countries', e.g. France, where SIs are enacted by agencies without ministerial – let alone parliamentary – involvement (personal communication from Ed Page).

MAJORITARIAN ADVANTAGES

The British political system is characterised by an extreme degree of majoritarianism, or as Arendt Lijphart (1984, 4) noted in a seminal study: 'The essence of the Westminster Model is majority rule.' Due to the FPP electoral system, it is usually the case that the governing party in Britain holds a majority of seats which is disproportionate to its share of the votes, hence the Laakso and Taagapera 'effective number of parties' measure is extremely low, between 2.1 and 2.3 (Laakso and Taagapera 1979, 3).

This means, *ceteris paribus*, that a government controlling a stable and disciplined majority is able to impose its will on Parliament. One particular institutional factor is responsible for this: the Chief Whip.

While Whips are known from other polities – e.g. the United States – they have a much more modest role. The Chief Whip resides at 9 Downing Street (formerly No. 12). While her official title is the rather modest 'Parliamentary Secretary to the Treasury', the Chief Whip has the power to justify that residence: she advises the Prime Minister on both appointments to the front bench and demotions and exercises the ultimate sanction of *de-selection* – a process proceeded by the 'removal of the whip' from the MP in question (temporary banishment from the parliamentary party).

It is beyond the scope of this chapter to consider the powers of the Chief Whip in detail, although it is difficult to overestimate her importance for maintaining party unity and, hence, for executive dominance (Lijphart 1999, 133). This institutional factor gives government a strongly partisan advantage. However, much as governments enjoy an advantage bestowed by the 'rules of the game', cultural factors cannot be discounted. As the Modernisation Committee (2001–2002, Second Report, 68) noted:

> All sides should be willing to abandon entrenched positions. Governments should accept that better scrutiny can produce better legislation. Oppositions should not mistake obstructionism for effective scrutiny. These though are matters of political culture. They cannot be resolved by amending the rules of procedure.

Conclusion

'Your business is not to govern the country', the Victorian Prime Minister William Gladstone told the Commons in 1869, 'but it is, if you think fit, to call to account those who do govern it' (quoted in Sampson 2004, 1). The UK Parliament has a proud tradition, but if the role of an elected assembly is to provide a check on the government of the day, it can no longer be considered a model for other nations. An 'arena parliament', the UK system gives the government a very privileged position *vis-à-vis* both the Lords and the Commons.

The reasons for this are partly historical: the events before and after the Civil War in the seventeenth century made the British wary of a strong legislature. And while, in the twentieth century, the Commons became the dominant House, the powers of the MPs are rather limited. Through the office of the Leader of the House government has a near total dominance over the parliamentary time-table (e.g. through guillotine motions and – since 1997 – programming motions). While the Lords can still upset the parliamentary time-table by delaying tactics, these powers have been considerably curtailed with the introduction of provisions for carry-over bills in 2002.

Unlike those of other polities, parliamentarians in the UK have the right to scrutinise secondary legislation. This has provided them with an opportunity to amend legislation, and have given them an influential – albeit a politically non-controversial – role.

Due to its electoral system, the UK has a low 'effective number of parties'. This – combined with a high level of party discipline (exercised through the Whips Office) – means that government has strong majoritarian–partisan advantages.

Britain may have one of the oldest Parliaments in the world, but not one of the strongest. If the health of a democracy is measured by its legislature's ability to hold the executive to account, the so-called mother of all parliaments may have a lot to learn from her daughters. Moreover, the weakness of the UK Parliament and its modest role as a deliberative chamber means that some of the claims regarding the superiority of representative democracy are exaggerated.

Part III

Case studies in citizen democracy

We have now acquired an understanding of the main processes of political participation: who votes, why they vote, what they vote for and sundry other activities. But politics in not an exact science! No matter how many statistics we study there will always be individual factors to be taken into account.

To understand politics is – as mentioned in chapter 1 – to engage in 'thick description', using case studies to understand the details that get lost in the grander theories. Hence, in Part III of this book I look at three case studies: the decision to hold referendums in the UK (chapter 8); what determines the outcome of referendums, using the examples of the votes on the European Constitution in 2005 (chapter 9); and postal voting (chapter 10).

The aim of these chapters is *not* to develop a grand theory, let alone to incorporate the facts into general political theories. They seek rather to provide a different – and complementary – perspective. As I said in the Introduction, the study of politics takes place at different levels of abstraction, and it is only by gaining an understanding of all of them that it becomes possible to engage in a study of politics based on what Wright Mills called 'the sociological imagination'.

The case studies also serve another purpose. By gaining an understanding of these cases, it becomes possible to combine theoretical insight and practical understanding, and hence assess reforms and proposed changes to the system.

8

Decisions to hold referendums in the UK

Beginning with a history of referendums in the UK, this chapter considers the process of the initiation of referendums in the UK. While referendums in the 1970s were held as a result of intra-party divisions (i.e. in order to avoid political splits), those held or proposed by the New Labour Government since 1996 seem to suggest that referendums are being used for a variety of reasons, including to give legitimacy to controversial decisions and to wrong-foot political opponents.

Referendums have become part of the constitutional tapestry of the UK. Proposed referendums on the European Constitution, the Euro and PR, and the actual referendums on the Good Friday Agreement, devolution in Scotland, Wales, London, and – most recently –in the north east of England, are but some of the examples of the growing use of direct democracy in a country whose 'distinctive contribution to civilisation', according to the *Daily Telegraph*, 'has been . . . institutions of representative government' (Editorial, 19 December 1997). This left precious little scope and taste for direct democracy. As Birch observed in the 1960s:

> It has occasionally been proposed that a referendum might be held on a particular issue, but the proposals do not appear to have been taken seriously. And there has been no support at all for the idea that the initiative and the referendum should be adopted as a permanent institution of government, as it is in Switzerland, so that the representatives could be by-passed. Views of this kind have found favour among peoples of British extraction in both Australia and the United States, but in Britain itself they have never acquired any kind of influence. (1964, 227–228)

A lot of water has passed beneath political bridges since the 1960s. Indeed, within 10 years of Birch's observation everything had changed. In 1973 a referendum was held on the future status of Northern Ireland, and in 1975 another on continued British membership of the EEC (the forerunner for the European Union).

As if to put a final nail into the coffin of pure representative government, yet another referendum was held in 1979 – on devolution (self-government) for Scotland and Wales. While no referendums were held during the years of Conservative rule (1979–1997), the greater use of referendums has continued since Tony Blair's New Labour was elected to power in 1997 (see box 8.1).

In addition to those listed in box 8.1, referendums have been in steady use at the local level. Since 2001 polls have been held by 31 local authorities on whether to have a directly elected mayor; by 2005 11 have been approved in such places as Stoke-on-Trent, Middlesbrough, Darlington and Watford (Batchelor 2005, 12) whereas they had been rejected in such places as Plymouth, Oxford, Gloucester, Berwick-on-Tweed and Kirklees (Electoral Commission 2002a). Moreover, a number

---

Box 8.1 *Major referendums in the UK*

Northern Ireland referendum, 1973, on whether Northern Ireland should remain part of the UK: Yes: 98.9%; No: 1.1%; turnout: 58.6% (The referendum was boycotted by the nationalist community).

United Kingdom referendum, 1975, on whether the UK should remain part of the European Community: Yes: 67.2%; No: 32.8%; turnout: 64.5%.

Scotland referendum, 1979, on whether there should be a Scottish Parliament: Yes: 51.6%; No: 48.4%; turnout: 63.8%.

Wales referendum, 1979, on whether there should be a Welsh Assembly: Yes: 20.3%; No: 79.7%; turnout: 58.8%.

Scotland referendum, 1997, two questions:

- Should there be a Scottish Parliament: Yes: 74.3%; No: 25.7%; turnout: 60.4%.
- Should a Scottish Parliament should have tax varying powers: Yes: 63.5%; No: 36.5%; turnout: 60.4%

Wales referendum, 1997, on whether there should be a Welsh Assembly: Yes: 50.3%; No: 49.7%; turnout: 50.1%.

London referendum, 1998, on whether there should be a Mayor of London and Greater London Authority: Yes: 72.0%; No: 28.0%; turnout: 34.1%.

Northern Ireland referendum, 1998, on the Good Friday Agreement: Yes: 71.1%; No: 29.9%; turnout: 81.0%.

North-east England referendum, 2004, on whether there should be an elected regional assembly: Yes: 22.1%; No: 77.9%; turnout: 47.7% (an all-postal vote).

Source: www.electoralcommission.org.uk/referendums (2004).

of local authorities have held special referendums on policy issues. Of particular interest are, perhaps, the three referendums held in Milton Keynes (1999), Bristol (2001) and Croydon (2001) on whether to increase local tax to improve public services. The results of the referendums have been mixed: voters in Bristol and Croydon voted for lower taxes; in Milton Keynes they opted for a tax increase. This is not a revolutionary development; indeed, in the early 1980s Secretary of State for the Environment Michael Heseltine advocated local referendums on tax policies. However, the idea was dropped after backbench opposition and following results that went against the Conservative Government's political preferences (Lee 1986).

Another in the same category was the 2005 referendum on a congestion charge in Edinburgh (which was overwhelmingly defeated by 62 per cent). Unlike national referendums, local referendums are fairly well established in the British political tradition. Since the 1850s there have been provisions for local polls (e.g. on free libraries), and from 1858 to 1974 it was possible for citizens to demand a poll on decisions made by local councils (Butler and Ranney 1978). In addition to these provisions for local referendums, Wales had (until 2002) provisions for referendums on the Sunday opening of public houses.

The history of the referendum in Britain since 1945

Taking stock after the Blair Government's first spate of constitutional reforms in the late 1990s, the Labour MP Tony Wright (2003, 30) concluded – almost as an afterthought – 'and referendums became the established vehicles for approving constitutional change'. It is, perhaps, indicative of the status of the referendum in the British Constitution that only a few years earlier the referendum had been regarded constitutionally unpalatable. As recently as 1992, the Conservative Foreign Office Minister Tristan Garel-Jones said in the Commons debate over the Maastricht Treaty that the referendum was 'an abdication of the responsibility of the House and of the Government of the day' (*House of Commons Debates*, Vol. 204, 21 February 1992, col. 627).

As only Labour governments have made use of the referendum, it is tempting to see the disagreement between Garel-Jones and Wright as an indication of a partisan divide over the referendum, with Labour being more referendum-friendly than the Tories. This is far from being the case. Indeed, it is noteworthy that the Labour Prime Minister Harold Wilson argued along the very same lines as did Garel-Jones in a debate in the House of Commons in 1966. Mr Wilson rejected the very idea of the referendum, on the grounds that 'decisions of great moment of this kind have to be taken by the elected government of the day, responsible to this House. The constitutional position is that whatever this House decides on this matter, or any other matter, is the right decision' (*House of Commons Debates*, Vol. 731, 14 July 1966, col. 1718).

Dicey and the political theory of the referendum

Wilson's position, then, was not surprising. It is, in fact, interesting, from a historical point of view, that the Labour Party – despite its use of the referendum in the 1970s and the 1990s – has traditionally been ideologically opposed to submitting issues to the voters.

The reason for this opposition is, it seems, largely historically determined. The referendum was originally championed by liberal Unionists who advocated a referendum on Irish Home Rule in the 1890s, i.e. by conservatives who sought to resist the very changes and reforms that the 'progressive' parties pursued. One theoretician – above all – is credited with making a theoretical case for the referendum: A.V. Dicey – ironically the constitutional theorist traditionally associated with the notion of the sovereignty of Parliament!

The fundamental problem for the liberal Unionists was that, although the majority of voters favoured the Liberal Party over the Conservatives, it seemed that an even larger majority was opposed to Gladstone's policy of granting devolution to Ireland. A referendum, believed Dicey, would partly rectify this situation. As he wrote in a letter to fellow-unionist J. St Loe Strachey:

> I value the referendum first because it is doing away with the strictly speaking absurd system which at present exists, of acting on the presumption that electors can best answer the question raised, e.g. by Home Rule, when it is put together with totally different questions . . . and secondly because [it] is an emphatic assertion of the principle that nation stands above parties. (Quoted in Cosgrove 1981, 108)

The referendum, according to Dicey, would rectify this problem by being 'nothing more or nothing less than a national veto' (Dicey in ibid,, 106), i.e. a mechanism which can 'delay or forbid innovations condemned by the weight both of the uneducated and the educated opinion' (Dicey 1982, cxi).

To historians of political thought this use of direct democracy was hardly novel. No less a political thinker than Niccoló Machiavelli had made the same case for – in McCormick's words – 'controlling elites with ferocious populism' (McCormick 2001, 1190). So too, of course, did Rousseau (Qvortrup 2003). What was new was that Dicey and others outlined how the referendum could be made compatible with a modern system of representative government.

Under the proposal developed by Dicey, the referendum would complement rather than replace representative government. Dicey proposed the introduction of a Referendum Act which would require a referendum before fundamental changes to the Constitution could be enacted (see Qvortrup 1999). Through such an Act it would be possible to guard 'the rights of the nation against the usurpation of national authority of any party which happens to have a parliamentary majority' (Dicey to Lord Salisbury, quoted in Cosgrove 1981, 106). As Dicey saw it, such an act would – as a by-product – facilitate a more responsible system of representative government:

> If it was certain that the ultimate fate of a measure . . . would finally turn not upon the votes of members in Parliament, but on voters outside who never took part in the hollow and artificial warfare waged at Westminster, it is conceivable that speakers in Parliament might address themselves to the task of convincing an unseen audience [and] conceivable . . . that the power of reasoning might become a force of some slight moment even in practical politics. (1890, 503)

In other words, the mere threat of a referendum would encourage the elected politicians to listen to their constituents; referendums would strengthen representative democracy.

The referendum in practice

While no referendum was held until the 1970s, the idea of the referendum was – at times – official Conservative policy: in the constitutional debate of 1910, Conservative leader Arthur Balfour proposed that the referendum be used to settle the dispute between the Lords and the Commons, as well as the Tories later proposed that the vexed issue of tariff reform was submitted to a vote among all the electors.

Yet, as expected, not everyone was in favour of arresting change. In particular the Liberals and the Labour Party (being the architects of large-scale reforms) dismissed the Conservative (*sic!*) case for the referendum. It was not surprising, therefore, that Clement Atlee rejected Winston Churchill's proposed referendum on the continuation of the war-time coalition in 1945 (Bogdanor 1994, 36).

That the Labour Party – historically a party critical of the device – adopted the referendum in the 1970s cannot be said to be due to the party's ideological baggage; rather the change of heart seems to be a result of political expediency rather than the consequence of principled

considerations. As noted above, Harold Wilson was critical of the referendum on the EEC while Labour was in government in the 1960s.
However, matters changed after Labour lost the 1970 general election.

Being in opposition in 1972, when the Conservative Government
under Ted Heath took Britain into the EEC, the majority of the Labour
Party's MPs followed the party line and voted against UK membership.
Yet, a significant group within the party, including Shadow Chancellor
of the Exchequer Roy Jenkins, led a rebellion and voted with the
Conservative Government. This posed a problem for the Labour Party.
Aspiring to get back into power – and capitalising on the increasingly
unpopular Conservative Government's decline in the polls – Labour
needed to show that it was capable of governing without being ham-
pered by damaging internal spits over policies.

The referendum proved to be the device that rescued the Labour Party.
By agreeing to disagree, the party could claim that a vote for Labour
would not – at least not automatically – be a vote for withdrawal from
the EEC. The people would be given a choice; they would, politically
speaking, be allowed to have their cake and eat it: they could vote for a
party at a general election and – if they so chose – vote against this
party's policy at a later date.

As the leading Labour politician Jim Callaghan (Prime Minister
1976–1979) observed, the referendum (to which he had previously
been opposed) would be 'a rubber life raft into which the whole party
will one day have to climb' (quoted in Butler and Kitzinger 1975, 12).
Or, as it was put by his colleague – and rival – Tony Benn: 'a referendum
would get it [the European issue] out of our system and leave the party
united: the party was divided at this stage and we should accept the fact
that this would resolve it' (Benn quoted in Wright et al. 2000, 145).

When the issue of continued membership eventually was submitted
to the voters in June 1975, the Labour leadership had changed course.
Having been opposed to UK membership while in opposition, the party
leadership now supported it – with the exception of some (mostly) left-
leaning members of the Cabinet, most notably Tony Benn, Peter Shore,
Michael Foot and Barbara Castle. In the vote on 5 June 1975, an overwhelming majority of 17 million voted for continued membership; only
8 million voted to leave.

Why referendums: mediating device or electoral tactics?

A case could be – and indeed has been – made for saying that the
1975 referendum followed a pattern identified by Norwegian political
scientist Tor Bjørklund. According to Bjørklund, referendums are the

result of political parties' attempts to paper over internal splits over 'valency issues', i.e. issues of peripheral importance to the parties in question. Analyzing Scandinavian referendums in the 1970s, Bjørklund concluded that 'a government [or party], which is divided on an important issue . . . may embrace the referendum as a mediating device' (1982, 248).

There is a lot to be said for this interpretation when analysing the decision to submit the 'European' issue to a referendum in Britain in 1975. The question remains, however, whether Bjørklund's model, while theoretically stringent, is not too parsimonious. Other referendums held subsequently do not – on the face of it – seem to support Bjørklund's model. Rather than trying to fit the initiation of referendums into a rigid model, it seems more productive to work with a taxonomy that acknowledges that referendums may be called for many different reasons. Such a model has been developed by Laurence Morel (2001). Slightly elaborating on Morel's model we can distinguish between:

• *Decision-solving referendums*: proposals for referendums when a government is split over an issue. The classic example is the Norwegian Labour Government in 1971, which – when faced with a damaging split of the party – decide to resolve the issue of continued Norwegian membership of the EEC (the forerunner of the EU) by submitting the issue to the voters.
• *Legislative referendums*: proposals for a referendum called by a minority government in order to bypass a parliamentary majority. A classic example was French President Charles de Gaulle's decision to submit his proposal for direct election of the president when he failed to win support for his proposal in the National Assembly.
• *Strategic referendums*: a typical example could be Californian Governor Pete Wilson's use of Proposition 189 (an anti-immigration measure) to win support for a second term.
• *Legitimation referendums*: referendums on controversial issues which require direct legitimation by the people. An example was the decision to submit the issue of Swedish membership of the Euro to a referendum in 2003.
• *Politically obligatory referendums*: referendums on controversial political issues, where the executive is politically obligated to submit the issue to the voters for fear of an electoral backlash, e.g. the Danish Government's decision to hold a referendum on the Edinburgh Agreement (the Danes' four opt-outs of the Maastricht Treaty) in 1993.

How do the British referendums fit the bill – or do they? The 1975 referendum, as we have seen, was used specifically as a mediating device:
it was a 'decision-solving referendum'. The same – or so it might be
argued – was true in the case of the referendum on Scottish and Welsh
devolution. In the latter case, large sections of the Labour Party's back-
benchers opposed the Government's policy to establish devolved parliaments in the two nations. To fend off another split the Government
grudgingly accepted that the policies were submitted to referendums in
the two nations (both of which were lost – though in the case of Scotland
only because the number of Yes votes did not constitute the required 40
per cent of the eligible voters).

On closer scrutiny, however, this categorisation fails to appreciate the
nuances of the debate leading up to the referendum. The decision to
hold a referendum was rather by default – not by design. Bjørklund once
noted that 'those whose standpoint would be voted down if it went
through the channels of representative democracy can embrace the
demand for a referendum on the issue. In the absence of a referendum
the battle is lost' (1982: 247).

This was exactly the situation of the anti-devolutionists. The Scotland
and Wales Devolution Bill (which was introduced into the Commons in
1976) did not include provisions for a referendum at all, ostensibly
because the Government underestimated the opposition to the bill from
Labour backbenchers, who were, in Vernon Bogdanor's words, 'unen-
thusiastic, if not positively hostile, to devolution' (1996, 227).

While opposed to devolution, the anti-devolutionists were anxious
not to bring down the Government by defeating the devolution proposals they consequently demanded a referendum before the legislation
received royal assent. This prompted the Government to withdraw the
Bill in favour of two separate Bills (introduced in November 1977), both
of which contained provisions for consultative referendums.

At this time, however, it had become clear that a parliamentary defeat
for the devolution Bills would result in the dismissal of the Callaghan
Government. This meant that the Labour opponents of devolution had
to devise new ways of inflicting damage on the proposals, without actually preventing their passage through Parliament. To achieve this aim,
George Cunningham, a Scot elected in an English constituency, tabled
an amendment stipulating that the proposal – once it was approved by
Parliament – had to be supported by at least 40 per cent of the eligible
voters in each of the two nations.

That the Callaghan Government eventually was defeated in a no-
confidence motion – after the referendums had failed – is not the fundamental lesson to be drawn for the purposes of this analysis. Indeed, it is

relatively rare that governments resign when they suffer defeats in referendums – the defeats of referendums on the Euro in Denmark and Sweden in 2000 and 2003 did not have that result (Qvortrup 2005, 60). What we are interested in is rather *why* the referendums were called in the first place.

Unlike plebiscite in 1975, the 1979 referendum was not embraced as a mediating device; rather the decision to submit the issue to the voters came about as a result of the dynamics associated with – what Laurence Morel calls – an 'opposition referendum' (2001, 2005). A minority within the Labour Party used its 'blackmail potential' (Sartori 1976). The decision was not, as in the early 1970s, an agreement to disagree; rather the Government was forced to make concessions for fear of failing to win parliamentary approval for the Bills. Yet, as with the referendum on the EEC, the decision to hold a referendum on devolution was taken to ensure that the Labour Party avoided a damaging split (in the event only one MP, the Scottish pro-devolutionist Jim Sillars, left the Labour Party, eventually to join the Scottish Nationalist Party).

While Bjørklund's analysis of the Scandinavian votes in the 1970s conformed to his theory that referendums are mediating devices embraced to avoid splits within governments, coalitions, or parties, the more recent referendums in that part of the world have not supported the Bjørklund's theory. The Norwegian Government and the parties supporting it were not split over the issue of EU membership in the early 1990s; nor was the Swedish Government. The 1994 vote 'was . . . not preceded by any conscious decision at all, a mandatory referendum on the EU issue being by this time in effect a silent dimension of the political system' (Wyller 1996: 142). It would seem, in other words, that the decision to call referendums in Scandinavia (with Denmark as the possible exception, as referendums in that country are constitutionally mandated) had become a convention of the Constitution: they were 'politically obligatory referendums' (Morel 2001).

The decision to hold a referendum on the EU Constitution

A similar analysis, it might be argued, could be made of the decision to hold a referendum in the UK on the European Constitution. Having been on the back foot over the issue of a referendum, Blair bowed to political pressure and declared in April 2004 that Britain would not ratify the European Constitution unless it had received the approval of the majority in a referendum. But why? Perhaps because the referendum was politically obligatory!

Before coming to power Blair had expressed support for a 'greater use of referendums'. The referendum 'gives citizens a veto over proposals to change their system of government' (Blair 1996, 34). His apparent commitment to politically obligatory referendums was no passing fancy: in 1994 he had acknowledged that in the event of 'a major constitutional change there clearly is a case for ensuring that the decision can be . . . taken by the British people (*Sunday Telegraph*, 11 December 1994). Other cabinet ministers were less pronounced in their enthusiasm, although David Blunkett, Jack Straw and Robin Cook on several occasions have voiced their support for referendums. Interestingly Gordon Brown has not commented favourably or otherwise on referendums!

Once in office Blair's enthusiasm for referendums cooled, which perhaps is hardly surprising: after all, as Lijphart once observed, 'when governments control the referendum, they will tend to use it only when they expect to win' (1984, 203). After the referendums in 1997–1998 (on devolution in Scotland and Wales and on the Good Friday Agreement in Northern Ireland) no others were held – or proposed – until 2004. It seemed that the referendum had suffered the same fate as in the late 1970s, when the Tories had (momentarily) toyed with the idea of letting the people have a greater say over their own affairs.

In opposition, the Tory leader Margaret Thatcher had championed the referendum. In the words of a *Sun* editorial (14 October 1977): 'Margaret Thatcher has left no senior colleague in doubt that she regards the referendum itself as both a necessary constitutional development and a potential vote winner . . . it begins to look as if the referendum, once considered an alien political device, may now be an idea whose time has come in Britain'. However, once in office, Thatcher realised that she did not need the referendum to implement trade union reforms, rejecting all calls for a plebiscite.

Blair's attitude to the referendum seems to have followed the same trajectory as had Thatcher's. Having used the device in the first few years of his reign, Blair now sounded the familiar opposition to the referendum. However, it seems that Blair – having unleashed the referendum spectre early in his tenure – was in a different position from Thatcher's in that it was difficult for him not to bow to pressure for a referendum. To illustrate this we might consider the case of the decision to hold a referendum on the European Constitution.

During the negotiations over the European Constitution, Blair had been opposed to holding a referendum. However, on 20 April Blair suddenly changed his tune and proposed such a referendum. Foreign Secretary Jack Straw emphasised the principled aspect: 'If you are in democratic politics, you have to take account of what people are thinking and you have to keep listening to people, and parties which don't do that fail badly' (BBC1, *News At Six*, 20 April 2004). However, Straw did not explain why his party, less than a week earlier, had take the opposite position.

Analysing political motivations is a complex and difficult task as we cannot be certain about a politician's motivation. In analysing Blair's decisions we must go behind the facade and try – in so far as we can – to patch together a narrative. So why did Blair change his mind? To answer that question it is necessary to understand the political context of the decision to hold a referendum. The war in Iraq had significantly weakened the Prime Minister's credibility. Moreover, the Conservative Party had successfully made the ratification of the European Constitution its central campaign theme in the run-up to the European parliamentary election. This proved problematical to Blair as opinion polls consistently showed that more than 70 per cent of the voters were opposed to the European Constitution. As a result of this, Blair's Downing Street political advisors and a number of cabinet ministers had considered their options. Unlike earlier, Blair faced three problems:

- the fact that the Conservative Party had become a genuine threat to Labour's election chances (it was within three points of Labour in the polls);
- the increasing chorus of attack on Blair from within his own camp over his failure to take on the Eurosceptics, and;
- Blair's growing concern about his place in history, i.e. his fear of being remembered only for the unpopular war in Iraq.

Faced with these challenges the Prime Minister had three options. He could:

1 force a constitution bill through Parliament before the next election;
2 seek a mandate for ratification of the European Constitution in a general election; or
3 call a referendum on the issue.

To force a referendum through Parliament would be a high-risk option for the Government. Announcing ratifying legislation in the November 2004 Queen's Speech would allow it time to try and buy-off potential Labour rebels in the Commons, as well as the Liberal Democrats and cross-benchers in the Lords. However, it was far from clear that the Bill would face an easy passage in both Houses, with a high-profile and growing backbench rebellion in the Commons and a likely majority in favour of a referendum amendment in the Lords. It seemed inevitable that the Government would have to resort to desperate measures, including aggressive whipping of rebel backbenchers, creating more Labour peers or curtailing the powers of the Lords. The political outcry that this would cause for a Government fighting hard to hold on to public opinion during the run-up to an election could be difficult to contain.

Given the already considerable unpopularity of the Government over the war in Iraq, any distraction from its positive messages (i.e. the healthy economy) was unwelcome. A speedy ratification was not an option. If a referendum was to be avoided, Blair would have to include the ratification of the Treaty in the Labour Manifesto.

A mandate in a general election seemed difficult to obtain, however, as 9 out of 10 voters supported calls for a referendum. Fighting the election without a referendum commitment would not be popular among Labour MPs facing challenges from pro-referendum Conservative and Liberal Democrat candidates in keenly fought marginal seats. Further, almost sixty Labour MPs were already known to be pro-referendum, and their number would probably rise during an election. To add to this, the pro-referendum MPs were mainly in safer seats, and therefore at less risk during an election, so that it would be *loyal* – anti-referendum – MPs who would suffer for not committing to a referendum.

Given these considerations it seems that Blair had no option but to let the voters decide. In short, while a referendum was not politically desirable, it *was* politically necessary. Can we therefore conclude that British referendums have become 'politically obligatory referendums' rather than 'decision-solving referendums'? Not entirely. The problem with political science is that it defies simplicity and neat categorisations.

Blair's other referendums

The decision to hold a referendum on the European Constitution was rather different from other decisions to hold referendums.

While in opposition the Labour party had been split over whether to support the introduction of PR. With a Cabinet split down the middle, it was agreed – before the 1997 election – that a referendum should be held on the issue before a change would take place. While archival evidence would be needed to draw a definite conclusion, a strong case can be made that the decision to submit the issue of electoral reform to the voters was a case of a *decision-solving referendum*. As in 1975, the party was split and the issue could be resolved by letting the voters decide (see the analysis of this in Qvortrup 2005, 61).

However, this rather neat explanation does not necessarily hold true for the other decisions to let the voters resolve the matter, such as in the cases of the referendums in north-east England in 2004 (Regional Assembly), in London in 1998 (directly elected mayor and an Assembly for London), the 1998 referendum in Northern Ireland (Good Friday Agreement), and indeed, the referendums in Scotland and Wales (devolution and tax-varying powers in Scotland).

As I have said, a complete analysis of the reasons for holding these referendums would require extensive archival study. For reasons to be briefly outlined below, these referendums can be classified as, respectively:

- *legitimation* referendums: north-east England, Government of London;
- *strategic* referendums: Scottish and Welsh devolution; introduction of the Euro; and
- *politically obligatory* referendums: Good Friday Agreement.

The decision to hold referendums – as I have argued at length elsewhere (ibid., 65) – was largely tactical. The Conservative Government of John Major had successfully argued that a vote for the Labour Party would be a vote for the break-up of the UK and for the introduction of higher taxes in Scotland (as the proposed Scottish Assembly was to be given tax-varying powers of 3p in the pound). To embarrass Labour, Michael Forsyth, the Secretary of State for Scotland, had challenged Labour to hold a referendum on the issue; something which the Shadow Secretary of State George Robertson had refused, arguing that devolution was the settled will of the Scottish people. However, in June 1996, on the very day when John Major was to give a speech challenging Labour, Peter Mandelson – the politician responsible for Labour's strategy – leaked a story to the *Scotsman* according to which Labour would hold referendums on devolution for both Scotland and Wales, as well as a separate referendum on tax-varying powers in Scotland. By doing so Labour regained the moral high ground, as the Conservatives were unwilling to consider a referendum, let alone contemplate the introduction of devolution, although opinion polls in both Scotland and Wales showed support for this.

The same pattern was repeated later that year, when the Conservative Party performed a political *volte face* by deciding to hold a referendum before the UK joined the Euro. This momentarily forced the Opposition on the defensive, although it decided soon after to follow suit and announce that a Labour government would take Britain into the Euro only following the endorsement of the British public in a referendum.

The logic behind the decision to hold referendums on a directly elected Assembly in the north east and on the introduction of an elected mayor and an Assembly for London, however, followed a different – and much less controversial – pattern. In 1995 a consultation document on regional government in England, *A Choice for England*, had – almost in passing – stated that there was a 'need for consent' by the voters before directly elected assemblies could be introduced (quoted in Gay, Winetrobe and Wood 1997, 49). This (*thin*) commitment – seemingly for the sake of consistency (Pimlot and Rao 2002, 68) – found its way into the consultation paper *A Voice for London*, published a few months later. According to the latter, 'the final plans for this authority could be subject to a confirmatory test of public consent such as a referendum. This would strengthen the position of the new authority by demonstrating that it had the active support of Londoners' (quoted in Gay, Winetrobe and Wood 1997, 28). This proposal was adopted by the Labour–Liberal Democrat Consultative Committee on Constitutional Reform prior to the 1997 election (ibid., 49).

Having decided to hold a referendum on London's system of government, as well as having held referendums on devolution in Scotland and Wales, it was difficult for John Prescott, the minister in charge of regional affairs, to abandon the idea of referendums prior to the introduction of regional assemblies. It was seemingly for this reason – rather than for principled or tactical reasons – that the Labour Government decided to hold referendums on regional assemblies. However, it should not be overlooked that the dwindling support for regional assemblies gradually made such referendums constitutionally necessary. Having initially planned referendums in the north east, Yorkshire and Humber, as well as in north-west England, public opposition forced the Government to scale down its commitment. In July 2004, consequently, John Prescott announced that the referendums in the north west and Yorkshire–Humber were to be postponed, and that only one referendum would be held.

It is difficult to fit this referendum into Morel's categories; and were we to squeeze the decision to hold referendums into her framework, it would probably be under legitimation referendums.

The decision to submit the Good Friday Agreement to a referendum in 1998 was a different kettle of political fish. In 1973 Prime Minister Edward Heath's Conservative Government had organised a referendum, the so-called 'Border Poll', asking voters to choose between remaining in the UK or joining the Republic of Ireland. Boycotted by the nationalist (and largely Catholic) community, the referendum – if anything – exacerbated the conflict in the province, and the referendum was generally seen as a fiasco (see chapter 4). Yet this unfortunate experience did not preclude the British and the Irish Government from using referendums altogether. Thus in the Anglo-Irish Agreement of 1986 it was stated that the status of Northern Ireland should not be altered unless proposals for constitutional changes were supported by a majority in a referendum. This policy, initiated by the Conservative Government, was adopted by the Labour Party. Eschewing a referendum on the Good Friday Agreement was never an option: it was politically obligatory in the strongest sense.

Conclusion

'The referendum had more to do with political expediency than constitutional principle or democracy' was the conclusion of Dennis Kavanagh's analysis (1996, 60) of the referendums held in Britain in the 1970s. The same conclusion, it seems, can be drawn as regards the British referendums initiated and held in the late 1990s.

Whereas the referendums of the 1970s seem to conform to Bjørklund's model, the referendum on the European Constitution was held as a result of considerations other than internal party unity. Rather than following a kind of natural law of referendum occurrence – as hinted at by Bjørklund – the distinguishing feature of the 1990s referendums was that they were a result of specific tactical and political considerations. In sum, the referendums held in Britain can – using an elaborated version of Morel's classification of referendums – be categorised as:

- *decision-solving* referendums: membership of the EEC (1975) and the Labour Party's decision to hold a referendum on a possible change to the electoral system;
- *legislative referendums*: referendums on devolution for Scotland and Wales (1979);
- *strategic* referendums: Scottish and Welsh devolution (1997); joining the Euro;
- *legitimation* referendums: directly elected mayor and an assembly for London 1998; regional assembly for the north east (2004);
- *politically obligatory* referendums: the Good-Friday Agreement and the European Constitution (2004).

In all these cases the referendum was a means of solving a problem.

But whatever one thinks about these uses of the referendum (and it should be obvious that ideals of public participation were not paramount), it seems beyond any reasonable doubt that the referendum has become part of the British Constitution; that Birch's 1964 assertion – 'there has been no support at all for the idea that the initiative and the referendum should be adopted as a permanent institution of government' – is no longer accurate. As Tocqueville noted: 'A new political science is needed for a world in itself quite new' (1988, 62).

9

Voting by the people: the referendums on the European Constitution

Having looked at how the decision to hold referendums is made, and having concluded that it reflects political opportunism rather than idealism, the question is whether such public consultations enable the voters to have a choice. Some writers have been sceptical, arguing that referendums, in reality, always result in a verdict that supports the ruling elite (e.g. Lijphart 1984). Indeed, the philosopher Michael Oakeshott noted:

> The plebiscite is not a method by which mass man imposes his choice upon his rulers; it's a method for generating a government with unlimited authority to make choices on his behalf. In the plebiscite the 'mass man' achieved final release from the burden of individuality: he was emphatically told what to choose. (1991, 380)

The question is, however, *did* 'mass man' do as he was told? This assertion can be tested by the following case studies of the 2005 referendums on the European Constitution in Spain, France, the Netherlands and Luxembourg.

On 20 February 2005, with 76.7 per cent of the voters in favour, Spanish electors supported the ratification of the European Constitution on a 42.2 per cent turnout. A few months later, on 29 May 2005, a majority (54.8 per cent) of the French voters rejected the same treaty on a 69.7 per cent turnout. Three days later, a majority of the Dutch voters followed suit, when 61.5 per cent voted No on a 63.3 percent turnout. Roughly a month later – on 10 June – a majority of the voters in Luxembourg voted for the Treaty by a 55–45 per cent split on a 86.27 per cent turnout – in a country where voting is compulsory. In the wake of the referendums sundry speculations have been advanced as to the reason for the outcomes. Explanations have been advanced as to why the voters rejected the Constitution, and pundits and politicians alike have pondered the determinants of the results. This chapter presents an analysis of the referendums in the light of international research and seeks to determine if the referendums formed a general pattern.

The political background and the referendums

Apart from Spain (which entered the EC in 1986), the other three countries involved – the Netherlands, Luxembourg and France – were founder-members of the EU. The countries differ significantly in size, political tradition and, indeed, with respect to their use of the referendum. Before analysing the data it is necessary to briefly consider the political background to the referendum in each country.

Spain

While not uncommon, referendums are relatively rare in Spanish politics. Apart from regional referendums to establish *autonomias* (independent regions) in Galicia, the Basque Country, Andalusia and Catalonia between 1979 and 1981 (Rouke, Hiskes and Zirakzadeh 1992, 132), and the 2006 referendum on further autonomy for Catalonia, only three nationwide referendums have been held since the introduction of democracy. After Franco's death, referendums were held on a law to legitimise the regime – the so-called *Ley para la reforma political*. The popular approval of this law paved the way for another referendum on the new Constitution two years later (LeDuc 2003, 79).

Legitimation through mechanisms of direct democracy thus played a not insignificant part in the transition to democracy. One of the issues before, during and after the transition to democracy was the country's relations with the EEC and NATO. Spain joined the latter after Adolfo Suarez's conservative Government won a vote on membership in the *Cortes* in 1982. However, NATO membership was met with considerable resistance among the voters and in the Opposition, the socialist *Partido Socialista Obrero Español* (PSOE).

After his victory in the 1983 election, socialist Prime Minister Felipe Gonzales gradually became convinced that Spain should remain a member of NATO (LeDuc 2003, 79). Following his announcement of his changed position in 1984, Señor Gonzales promised a referendum. While the opposition's call for a boycott of the vote was partially successful, the result was seen largely as a vote of confidence for the socialist Prime Minister, who declared that he would resign should the outcome be a No vote (LeDuc 2003, 79).

Like the referendum in 1986, the 2005 plebiscite was held according to Article 92 of the Constitution, which allows the Prime Minister (formally the King) to call a referendum following a positive vote in the *Cortes* (Parliament). Yet, unlike in 1986, it was not immediately clear why a referendum should be held. Opinion polls suggested strong support for the European Constitution; indeed, according to

Table 9.1 National referendums in Spain, 1976–2005

Date	Subject	Turnout (%)	Yes vote (%)
20.2.2005	EU Constitution	42.32	76.73
12.3.1986	NATO membership	59.41	56.85
7.12.1978	Constitution	66.99	91.73
15.12.1976	Reform policies	77.72	97.36

Sources: http://c2d.unige.ch; 'La abstención, clave en el referéndum de la constitución europea', *El Pais*, 21 February 2005.

Eurobarometer 87 per cent of the Spanish electorate regarded themselves as EU citizens and 85 per cent believed that EU membership was good for Spain).

To a degree the decision to submit the issue to a referendum happened by default. The conservative Aznar Government had been an ardent critic of the initial proposal for the European Constitution, arguing that it did not give Spain its due recognition as a large country. To strengthen its negotiating position – but also mindful that it would be impossible to halt the drafting of the Constitution – Aznar had promised that a referendum would be held before Spain would ratify the Constitution. By promising a referendum, Aznar could argue that, without concessions, the Spanish voters might reject the Constitution. This pledge was also adopted by the Opposition, PSOE, in the run-up to the election in 2004.

Following his surprising victory in the election in March 2004 (following the Madrid bombings), Jose Luis Rodriguez Zapatero made clear his decision to consult the people:

> My intention, as we set out in the election manifesto . . . is to hold a referendum so that all Spanish citizens can express themselves about the new text of the constitution . . . I hope this referendum takes place as quickly as possible and that Spain will be among the first EU countries to ratify the constitution. (*El Mundo*, 11 July 2004)

Keen that Spain should be seen as a bell-wether state for a successful ratification process, Prime Minister Zapatero had initially proposed a referendum in November 2004. However, legal requirements under the election law made it necessary to postpone the referendum until February 2005. Further, the process was prolonged following negotiations between PSOE and the *Partido Popular*, or People's Party (PP), regarding the administrative aspects of the referendum. The PSOE had proposed that government funding be spent on a campaign for the Constitution, rather than merely on an information campaign. This was rejected by the Opposition.

France

Referendums are often debated, though less frequently held, in France. In 2003 the French Constitution was changed in a decentralised direction, and provisions were made for Corsica to hold a referendum on its future status. In the same year *Union pour la démocracie française* (UDF), the smaller of the two parties in the Coalition Government, called for a referendum on Prime Minister Raffarin's proposal for a changed pension system (Ysmal 2004, 1006). Referendums are thus part of the political discourse in France – though more often as threats than realities. The device can thus be said to be important in France, not for the actual number of referendums held, but because of the potential it has for challenging the authority of the elected politicians.

The referendum was used particularly in the early years of the Fifth Republic. Charles de Gaulle consulted the people in 1958, 1961, 1962 and in 1969, when he used the provision in Article 12 of the Constitution to, respectively, overcome opposition to the autonomy of Algeria and the Evian Agreement (pertaining to Algerian independence), and to ensure support for his plan for direct election of the Chief Executive. By doing so, de Gaulle was able to compensate for lack of a parliamentary majority by circumnavigating the legislature and going directly to the voters (Ysmal 2004, 1006). That even de Gaulle eventually fell following a failed referendum in 1969 is probably the best evidence of the importance of the referendum in the early years of the Fifth Republic.

Subsequent French referendums (i.e. after de Gaulle) have had a different genesis, as a result of changed political circumstances. In the referendums in 1972 (on EEC enlargement), in 1988 (on New Caledonia), in 1992 (on the Maastricht Treaty) and in 2001 (on the terms of the President's tenure), the plebiscites were held not to by-pass Parliament but to increase the support for and the legitimacy of the President. The 2005 referendum, by contrast, can be more aptly described as a 'politically obligatory' referendum (see Morel 2005 and chapter 8 of this book).

To understand why Chirac submitted the Constitution to a referendum it is important to consider parallel developments in the UK. Both the British and the French Government had rejected calls for a referendum until the spring of 2004. However, having been put on the back-foot on the issue by the Conservative Opposition in the run-up to the European Parliament elections in 2004, the Blair Government had succumbed to the pressure for a referendum. The British *volte-face* made Chirac's position untenable. Consequently, the President decided to call a referendum in accordance with Article 12 of the 1958 Constitution. In theory, Chirac could have avoided a referendum. Indeed, if the issue had

Table 9.2 National referendums in France under the Fifth Republic

Date	Subject	Yes (%)	No (%)	Turnout (%)
24.09.2000	Reduction of the Presidency to a five-year term	73.21	26.79	69.81
20.09.1992	Maastricht Treaty	51.05	48.95	30.31
06.11.1988	New Caledonia (new statute for)	80	20	63.11
23.04.1972	Enlargement of the EEC	68.32	31.68	39.76
27.04.1969	Regional government and the role of the Senate	47.59	52.41	19.87
28.10.1962	Direct election of the President	62.25	37.25	23.03
08.04.1962	Evian Agreement (on Algeria)	90.81	9.19	24.66
08.01.1961	Autonomy for Algeria	74.99	25.01	26.24
28.09.1958	Constitution of the Fifth Republic	82.60	17.40	19.37

Source: IPSOS 2005; Morel 2005.

come up a year before he probably would have done. However, his decision to call a referendum must also be seen in the context of domestic political developments. Early in 2003 the President enjoyed high ratings due to his popular stance on the Iraq War. Yet the summer of that year was characterised by a number of political gaffes and miscalculations. Above all, the President was severely criticised for his failure to act over – indeed speak about – the heat-wave in which an estimated 15,000 (mostly elderly) citizens died. In the light of this criticism, the President had little choice but to bow to public pressure for a referendum, especially as his chief opponent within the *Union pour un mouvement populaire* (UMP), Nicolas Sarkozy (the party's Chairman and Chirac's rival for the 2007 presidential candidature) was in favour of a referendum, as also were 74 per cent of the electors and a majority of the UMP voters (CSA Poll, 21–22 April 2005).

However, it would be inaccurate to see Chirac's decision as merely defensive. The fact that the socialists were divided on the Constitution – just like the parties on the Right had been on the Maastricht Treaty – gave the President an opportunity to split the Left by calling a referendum. Initially he seemed sure of winning it; that position – as we will see – changed.

The Netherlands

The debate about the introduction of the referendum has a long history in Dutch politics and is not to be looked at in isolation (Gilhuis 1981). Traditionally the Dutch political parties have been rather sceptical of elements of direct democracy, especially the larger parties: *Partij van de*

Arbeid (PvdA; Labour); *Christen Democratisch Appèl* (CDA; Christian Democrats); and *Volkspartij van Vrijheid en Democratie* (VVD; Liberals) (See Van Holsteyn 2005). Indeed the former leader of VVD devoted a whole essay to attacking the referendum as an institution which would 'sever the roots of democracy' (Geertsema 1987, 21). However, the small centrist party D66 has traditionally advocated a greater use of the mechanisms of direct democracy (Morel 1992).

While this support has previously been but a valence issue, it has increasingly become one of VVD's core issues, and indeed became one of the party's conditions for joining the Liberals and the Christian Democrats in the Coalition Government led by Jan-Peter Balkenende (CDA) in 2003. This enthusiasm for direct democracy was probably triggered by strong public support for referendums.

According to the *Dutch Parliamentary Election Study* (ICPSR 2003), 76 per cent of the respondents 'fully agreed' with the statement 'On some of the important decisions in our country voters should be able to vote by means of a so-called referendum' (Van Holsteyn 2005, 34). However, the political elites were less convinced. Previously, a constitutional amendment for an abrogative referendum (*het korrektives referendum*) had been proposed. This proposal was, however, rejected by the Senate (*Eerste Kamer*) in 1999 when Hans Weigel, former leader of VVD, cast his vote against the amendment, which, consequently 'failed to pass by one vote' (Andeweg and Irwin 2005, 87).

Unable to get the constitutional amendment through Parliament three MPs, Farah Karimi (GroenLinks), Niesco Dubbelboer (PvdA) and Boris Van Der Ham (D66) introduced a Private Members' Bill for a consultative referendum on the European Constitution. According to the Bill's explanatory memorandum the aim of the referendum was to 'enhance the legitimacy of the decision-making process of the Constitutional Treaty, by asking the advice of the citizens on the ratification via a national referendum' (Van Holsteyn 2005, 9). The Bill became law on 3 February 2005.

Luxembourg

Like its northern and more populous neighbour, the debate about the introduction of the referendum in Luxembourg was driven predominately by idealistic concerns, i.e. a belief in the intrinsic value of direct democracy to increase legitimacy. The decision to hold a referendum in Luxembourg – like that taken in the Netherlands – was a product less of debates about the European Constitution than it was part of a general movement towards direct democracy. In 2003, the Chamber of Deputies had voted to change the Constitution. Whereas constitutional amendments and changes previously had to be supported by a two-thirds' majority of the deputies voting with a quorum of three-quarters of them, the new procedure did away with the quorum. Instead, it included a provision for referendums on proposed constitutional changes if demanded by one-quarter of the MPs or 25,000 voters (Dumond and Poirier 2004, 1070).

In addition to these changes, in 2003, Prime Minister Jean-Claude Juncker introduced a draft bill on popular initiative in legislation, which would allow 10,000 voters to initiate legislation to be voted on by the deputies. If these rejected a bill, a referendum on the proposal would be held if demanded by 25,000 voters. Further, the Government introduced a bill to implement the previously unimplemented Article 51 of the 1919 Constitution, which allowed for referendums. According to the draft Bill, a referendum should be held on a bill or an international treaty if supported by a two-thirds' majority of the deputies.

While no votes were taken on these proposals (they were not seen as pressing concerns at a time of low economic growth), the Council of the Government decided 'by order in council' that a referendum would be held on the European Constitution. This was the first referendum in the country since 1937 (Dumont and de Winter 2003, 474).

The campaigns

Spain

The Spanish referendum was characterised by a high degree of elite unity. The governing PSOE and the main opposition party, PP, campaigned for a Yes, as did the *Partido Nacionalista Vasco* and the Catalan equivalent *Convergéncia i Uno*. The opponents, by contrast, were a political rag-bag of mostly left-wing parties, such as the United Left party *Izquierda Unida*, *Esquerra Republicana de Catalunya*, and the Basque nationalist social democratic *Eusko Alkartasuna*, as well as the CGT trade union.

This elite convergence is not in itself unique; indeed, the same pattern was observed in the Irish referendums, and in the Danish and Swedish referendums on the Euro, in, respectively, 2000 and 2003. Yet, whereas the latter two referendums were characterised by a considerable level of public debate, the Spanish referendum was characterised by an almost shocking degree of political apathy and – perhaps as a result thereof – by an astonishing degree of ignorance about the content of the Treaty (*El Mundo*, 1 February 2005). More alarmingly still, this ignorance appears to have deepened in the course of the campaign. According to a CIS poll in November 2004 there was a 'very low or low level of knowledge of the constitution'. An Opina poll on 2 February 2005 found that more than 60 per cent of the voters were lacking in knowledge, while the number of those with a high level of knowledge grow slightly during this period. According to CIS 7 per cent had a high knowledge in November (*El Mundo*, 16 November 2004); in February 2005 this figure was measured at 11 per cent.

Although this deficient public understanding of a complex constitutional issue would not have surprised thinkers like José Ortega y Gasset, who famously warned against the people's lack of knowledge in *La Rebelion de las Masas* (Ortega y Gasset 1937), empirical evidence in support of voter ignorance is limited. In, fact voters are generally well informed about the issues (Qvortrup 2005, 35). In any case, it is questionable whether it is necessary for the voters to have an encyclopaedic knowledge of the issues in order that they reach decisions that reflect their opinions. Indeed, Bowler and Donovan (1998) have found evidence to suggest that voters can make decisions that are consistent with their belief systems when they rely on cues and information shortcuts. Thus an endorsement by a well-known politician (or even a celebrity) can enable the voter to navigate without reading all the information about the issue. This insight was not lost on the pro-constitutionalists. The Yes campaign, hired celebrities (including Dutch former-FC Barcelona player Johan Cruyff) to read excerpts from the text in broadcasts. Further, it distributed 5 million copies of the Constitution with the Sunday papers the week before the vote.

It is difficult to gauge the effect of this campaign. Support for the Constitution had dropped from 70 per cent in June 2004 to slightly below 40 per cent in January 2005. In the following weeks support picked up to 45 percent, with the No vote support at a constant 8 per cent. What is perhaps most remarkable is that the number of undecided voters increased from 10 percent in June 2004 to 40 percent in January 2005 – this group dropped to 35 per cent during the campaign.

Given these figures it seems plausible that the Yes camp succeeded in appealing to the undecided, thus questioning the universal applicability of the assumption that undecided voters tend to vote No (Bowler and Donovan 1998, 43). However, the referendum failed to capture the minds of the voters. Indeed, the political classes (including the mass media) for most of January and February paid far more attention the future of the Basque Country than they did to the future of the EU. (The Basque nationalists had proposed a new constitutional settlement which would have granted the province a larger degree of autonomy, which amounted to near sovereignty.)

The referendum on the European Constitution hit the headlines only in mid-January when the foundation *Centro de Estudios Juridicos Tomás*

Moro and the organisation *Otra Democracia Es Posible* complained to the National Electoral Commission about what they saw as the Government's unfair use of public funds. In response to these complaints, the Commission ruled that the Government's campaign had not been purely informative, and banned several of its campaign slogans. Yet, in spite of ruling in favour of the complainants, the Commission did not enforce its decision. The No camp appealed the decision to the Supreme Court, which initially responded that it would require more than ten working days to consider the complaint. This would have meant that the Court's decision would not be available until after the referendum. Following protests, the Court agreed to consider the complaint within three working days. However, the Court did not find that the Electoral Commission was legally required to enforce it initial ruling.

The result of the referendum was a landslide victory for the Yes campaign: 76.73 voted for the Treaty. At only 42 per cent, however, the turnout was the lowest in any election or referendum since the restoration of democracy in 1977, and was a disappointment and an embarrassment for the Zapatero Government which had hoped to capitalise on an enthusiastic endorsement of the Constitution.

Like the referendum in the Netherlands (see below), the referendum was not legally binding on the Government, but it paved the way for parliamentary ratification of the constitutional treaty in the *Congreso de los Diputados* on 28 April 2005 (with 319 voting Yes), and in the *Senado* on 18 May (225 Yes against 6 No and one abstention). At this time the Constitution was still set for ratification by the end of the year. The French referendum later changed this.

France

While opposed by the usual suspects of the extreme Left and the – arguably even more extreme – Right, the European Constitution was supported by the governing UMP, its right-wing allies in the UDF and by the leadership of the PS. The opinion polls initially pointed towards a solid Yes majority as more than 60 per cent of those polled declared that they would vote in favour of the Constitution. Leading by a 64–36 per cent margin by September 2004, little suggested that the pro-constitutionalists were in serious danger of repeating the cliff-hanger result of 1992, let alone of losing the referendum.

This overwhelming majority was – albeit briefly – reduced in December when opponents of the Constitution within the PS (led by former Prime Minister Laurent Fabius) sought to reverse the pro-stance adopted by party leader Jean-Francois Hollande. However, Fabius and his faction lost the party's internal poll when 58 per cent of the members

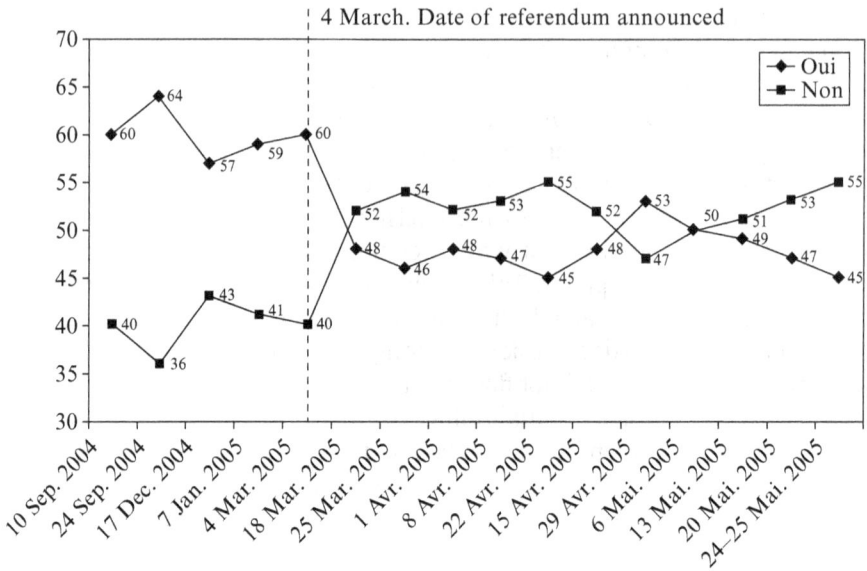

Figure 9.1   Voting intentions on the European Constitution
Source: IPSOS. Reproduced by Permission

voted for the Constitution on an 82 per cent turnout. (A similar vote
took place within the Green Party. On the 14 February a narrow majority of 52 per cent of the members voted in favour of the Constitution;
see *Le Monde*, 15 February 2005). Following this the gap between the
two sides in the opinion poll widened yet again.

When President Chirac set the date for the referendum on 4 March
2005, the Yes side was enjoying a 20 per cent lead. Within a mere two
weeks this lead had been reversed to a 4 percent lead for the opponents
of the Constitution. They held this lead, with the exception of a brief
reprieve for the pro-constitutionalists at the end of April.

Why this considerable turn-around? Were the voters swayed by the
arguments? And, if so, which arguments? It is impossible to say with certainty why the fortunes of a policy changes through a referendum campaign, but one factor often cited as important was the opposition to the
so-called Bolkestein Directive which was aimed at facilitating the free
movement of services throughout the EU. The directive aroused fears
about an influx of cheap labour from Central and Eastern Europe. And
while Chirac ensured that the directive was withdrawn, the theme of the
'Polish plumber' remained an Achilles heel for the pro-constitutionalists
– and a God-sent for the anti-constitutionalists, who played skilfully on

the voters' fears. In the week leading up to polling day, President Chirac tried – unsuccessfully – to appeal to the voters. The result on the 29 May seemed a foregone conclusion – and no one was too surprised by the outcome.

The Netherlands

The campaign in the Netherlands followed a somewhat different pattern. Whereas the French campaign was characterised by much media interest and intense debate, the Dutch referendum seemed almost a non-event. Perhaps because it had no previous experience with referendums, the Government misread the dynamic of a referendum campaign (where voting intentions are often shaped early in the campaign). As a result the Yes side (headed by Minister for Europe Atzo Nicolaï) left it to the No side to set the agenda for the debate. The No side was a motley crew of extreme left- and right-wing individuals, groups and organisations. The parties to the Left of PvdA, especially the socialists, emphasised that a Yes to the Constitution would jeopardise the Netherlands' liberal drug and social legislation. Furthermore – and perhaps surprisingly – the Left also emphasised nationalist themes, including that the Netherlands could become a province in a European super-state.

The sovereignty theme was, not surprisingly, the central plank in the campaign by the far Right, which was dominated by the List Pim Fortuyn and the Geert Wilders Group (a splinter group from the VVD formed by the far Right politician Geert Wilders who had left the VVD in protest against the party's support for Turkish membership of the EU). Wilders campaigned on the slogan 'The Netherlands must remain' (*Nederland moet blijven*), but also stressed that the adoption of the Constitution would lead to increased immigration, a 'threat' which he linked with Turkey's possible accession to the EU.

Having set the agenda, the Yes side found it difficult to make an adequate response. Instead of focusing on the larger themes and the need for the Constitution, the Government and the social democrats' campaigns were characterised by political fire-fighting. Increasingly desperate – as the polls pointed to a No vote – the pro-constitutionalists resorted to a campaign which can best be described as scaremongering. Minister for Economic Affairs Laurens Jan Brikhorst claimed that a No outcome would mean that 'the lights would go out for the Dutch economy', Foreign Minister Ben Bot, speculated that a no would lead to an economic down-turn, and – in a final intervention – VVD released a campaign video in which it suggested that a negative result would result in calamities and an uncertain future for Europe – indeed, they likened the consequences of a No to the Holocaust. The video was withdrawn, but it provided the No side with good arguments and a proof that the Yes lobby had panicked.

As in France, the result was a foregone conclusion several days ahead of the vote. The headline 'Poll: Netherlands Vote Against' (*Peilingen: ook Nederland stemt tegen*) in the newspaper *de Volkskrant* on 31 May merely said what everybody already knew: the country in which 76 per cent viewed the European Union as 'a good thing' (*Eurobarometer*, 62), an overwhelming majority had rejected the European Constitution.

Luxembourg

Whereas the Dutch often spoke of a gorge or gap (*kloof*) between the voters and the elite, that did not – initially – seem to describe the situation in Luxembourg. Like the parliamentary parties (the officially neutral ADR excepted), the vast majority of the citizens of Luxembourg have traditionally been among the most Europhile in the EU. Confident of winning the referendum, Jean-Claude Junker vowed that he would resign in the event of a No vote. This promise by the otherwise popular Prime Minister did not seem to have much impact on the voters: indeed, according to the Ilres Poll (April 2005), 45 per cent found that the resignation threat amounted to 'blackmail'.

Unlike in France, the interest in the referendum was limited – and people's knowledge of the Constitution even more modest. Only 8 per cent of the respondents in the Ilres Poll in April claimed to be well-informed about the Constitution, while a striking 81 per cent had either 'little' or 'no knowledge' of it. At this stage in the campaign, however, there was little to suggest that the referendum would be lost. This changed in the wake of the rejections of the Constitution in France and the Netherlands. At the time of the European Summit (20–30 June 2005) the two sides were within a whisker of one another.

Yet, unlike in France and the Netherlands, at no stage was the No lobby ahead. In the aftermath of the Summit the Juncker Government stepped up the campaign and, given the practically invisible opposition, managed to stabilise the lead and to increase its support. Yet Junker could not claim that the 56.52 per cent majority in favour of ratification was an endorsement, let alone a triumph. Although Luxembourg (like Belgium and Australia) has compulsory voting, only 86.27 percent turned out to vote.

Due to this low turnout the European Constitution was supported by less than half of the electorate (49.1 per cent) backed it. This in itself provides food for thought at a time when much political science is based on economic rationality: more than one in eight of the voters in the Arch

Duchy preferred paying the 500 Euro fine rather than making up their minds about the Constitution.

The referendum – which was intended as a celebration at the end of the country's six months at the helm (Luxembourg held the EU Presidency for the first half of 2005) turned out to be an embarrassment for the Juncker Government.

General patterns of referendum voting?

Could these results have been foreseen? Is there a pattern in referendum voting which would have enabled us to predict the fate of the Constitutional Treaty? Aleks Szczerbiak and Paul Taggart have suggested that referendums are determined by 'underlying mass attitudes in combination with cues determined by the elites' (Szczerbiak and Taggart 2004, 749). The Spanish case certainly seems to fit their thesis almost perfectly: a combination of underlying support for the EU and cues from opinion-formers (and celebrities) made the Yes result almost inevitable. Yet the same is less obvious for the other three referendums. There was no shortage of elite cues in France, the Netherlands and Luxembourg, and – according to *Eurobarometer* surveys – all the three countries' voters were among the most supportive of European integration. Given this, one would have expected endorsement of the Treaty in the Netherlands and France – and a higher level of support in Luxembourg.

An alternative explanation is the present author's model, which predicts that referendums tend to be won when an economy is in recession and when a government has taken office recently (Qvortrup 2005, 116).

It seems that this economic model might have some credence in the case of Luxembourg, where the voters supported the Constitution at a time of economic decline. Conversely, in the Netherlands the low growth and the relatively new Government should – according to this theory – have led to a Yes vote. The situation in the Netherlands was not markedly different from that of France. The economy – while not in dire crisis – was slumping. From 2002 onwards, it was clear that the 'the economic conditions were deteriorated' when compared to those of previous years (Lucardie and Voerman 2004, 1084). According to the theory this should have given the pro-constitutionalists an advantage. It is equally difficult to find evidence for the economic theory in the French referendum. Indeed, the French economy was in a crisis with chronic high unemployment and a considerable public debt-problem.

The theory that recently elected governments win referendums seems more plausible. Indeed, the Spanish referendum is an almost paradigmatic example of this. Further, as regards France, one could argue that the long-serving Chirac Government was one of the reasons for the No vote. Elected in 1995 and re-elected in 2002 (without much enthusiasm!), Chirac's Government was politically a lame political duck, who was seen as a liability. As the *Financial Times* (31 May 2005) wrote:

> It is difficult to recall anything positive about Jacques Chirac's 10 years in Office. Mr Chirac occupies the Elysée palace thanks to a freak landslide victory in 2002 when the French left was forced to support him to keep out Jean-Marie Le Pen, the Front National leader. The French president's support was borrowed, not earned and on Sunday many voters gleefully called in their loans.

Yet, neat though this explanation may seem it is too simplistic, even in the case of France, and it cannot account for the result in Luxembourg and the Netherlands. According to the 'new government' theory the voters in Luxembourg should have given the Treaty an electoral kicking. as Jean-Claude Juncker had been in office since 1995. Yet, they voted for the Treaty, though the margin was much smaller than expected as the pro-constitutionalists had a 40 per cent lead in October 2004 (IFES Market Research, October 2004). Moreover, the Dutch Government had been in office only since 2001, not long enough for it to lose credibility vis-à-vis the voting public.

So what then accounts for the results of the referendums? Did radically different, indeed, parochial factors produce them or was there a common denominator?

One often-cited factor for the results in France and the Netherlands was the unpopularity of the governments of those countries (in France, Prime Minister Raferin and President Chirac especially). French and Dutch politicians – so one argument runs – were to blame for the poor result: 'Chirac désavué' said the banner headline of *Le Monde* (31 May 2005). Can this view be supported by the statistical evidence?

If we consider the polls from France, it seems that support was actually strongest in the areas of greatest government popularity, e.g. in Paris and Ill de France. However, these were also the areas with the lowest turnout (*Le Figaro*, 31 May 2005).

This is a finding that goes against the conventional wisdom about campaigns. In both France and the Netherlands the results have been blamed on the unpopularity of, respectively, Jacques Chirac and Jan Peter Balkenende, just as the positive outcome in Luxembourg has been attributed to the popularity of PM Jean Claude Juncker. There is little statistical evidence to support this thesis. Indeed, the polls suggest that the Centre-Right voters generally supported the Constitution, whereas a majority of the socialist voters (supporters of, respectively, PS in France and PvdA in the Netherlands did not. We do not have figures for LSAP in Luxembourg and PSOE in Spain).

In France the overwhelming majority, 80 per cent, of the UMP voters supported the Constitution, i.e. Chirac successfully rallied his own party supporters, whereas Hollande (the PS leader), largely due to the split in the party, failed to get the support for the Constitution from his voters that he had secured in the internal party ballot in December. The failure of the referendum was not a result of Chirac's failure to appeal to his voters.

The UMP voters turned out in higher numbers (72 per cent) than the country as a whole and voted overwhelmingly for the Treaty. The Socialists turned out in slightly lower numbers (68 per cent) than the average turnout (69.7).

In the Netherlands, two of the government parties, D66 and CDA (Balkenende's party), supported the Treaty overwhelmingly (both 76 per cent), whereas the support was considerably lower among VVP voters, possibly reflecting the split in the party when Wilders resigned the whip. In the Netherlands, too, the result was largely due to a split among social democratic voters: PvdA – a pro-Constitution party – could persuade only 42 per cent of its voters to support the treaty.

There may be different psephological reasons for this, but one might be that the Constitution by and large was negotiated by Centre–Right governments (with the exception of Germany's). That the Constitution

Table 9.3 Party alignments and voting preference: France and the Netherlands

Political party	Yes (%)	No (%)
UMP (France)	80	20
PS (France)	44	56
Far Left (France): PCF, LO	6	94
Far Right (France): FN	7	93
CDA (Netherlands)	76	24
PvdA (Netherlands)	42	58
D66 (Netherlands)	76	24
VVP (Netherlands)	57	43
Far Left (Netherlands): Socialists	4	96
Far Right (Netherlands): Geert Wilders Group	4	96

Sources: IPSOS 2005; Maurice de Hond: www.peil.nl.

was the handiwork of right-leaning governments is likely to have created the impression among the left-leaning voters that the Constitution was a (more or less veiled) threat to the welfare state. Whereas in the 1980s and the 1990s, the integration process was driven forward by moderate socialists in the Jacques Delores mould, the steps towards 'ever closer union' is now mostly under the stewardship of (nominally) conservative governments. This is not likely to have endeared socialist voters to the EU.

The situation is thus the opposite of what it was in 1992, when the Maastricht Treaty nearly fell in France because the parties on the Right could not muster support for it – but when this was backed by the PS voters (Morel 1996).

There is still – notwithstanding Inglehart's post-materialist thesis – a correlation between income categories and voting behaviour. In the Netherlands 68 per cent of those in the lowest income groups voted No, whereas only 51 per cent of those in the highest income group voted No (www.peil.nl). In France the same tendency was in evidence: 79 per cent of those in the lowest income groups voted against the Treaty. Only 32 per cent of the functionaries did the same (SOFRES).

Comparative political scientists rely on information from different countries. Alas, we have insufficient data on Luxembourg to carry out a similar analysis. However, anecdotal evidence – as reported in the media – suggests that the LSAP voters in Luxembourg supported the treaty (*Le voix*, 13 July 2005). Just as in Spain, the social democrats in this, the smallest of the EU founding countries, thus succeeded where their opposite numbers in the Hague and Paris had failed.

That the outcome of the referendum turned on the support of the moderate left, i.e. that the No veto in the Netherlands and France was the result of a high level of opposition from among PvdA and PS voters, does not, of course, indicate that voters in other countries were motivated by the same factors. I have noted already that parties on the Dutch Left invoked nationalist rhetoric. Was this a common tendency?

The polls suggest that voters in the four countries had different reasons for reaching their decisions. In Luxembourg the main reason for voting No was the 'need for re-negotiation' (65 per cent) – the chief motivation for a Yes vote was 'support for the European project' (81 per cent), according to the Ilres Poll. In the Netherlands the chief motivation for voting against the Constitution was 'that the Netherlands pays too much to the EU' (62 per cent), followed by concern that the 'Netherlands will have less control over its own affairs' (56 per cent); conversely, the main reason for Dutch support of the Constitution was that 'Europe needs to tackle cross-border problems (Harmsen 2005). In France, the main reason for voting No was dissatisfaction with the economic situation (52 per cent), though 40 per cent found that it was 'too economically liberal' ('trop libérale sur le plan économique').

Survey specialists might argue that these figures are incompatible – and (technically speaking) rightly so! A truly scientific study would have asked the same questions of all the countries. However, there is – presumably – a reason why those questions were asked. The surveys were not conducted in a vacuum, but reflected the debate in each of the countries. And because that debate varied from country to country, the pollsters asked different questions. This is itself an important finding – though it may appear trivial. For the fact that the four countries had different debates about the Constitution shows that Europe has not yet developed a transnational discourse, as has been the hope of radical democrats like Jürgen Habermas.

The immediate aftermath: consequences of the No

The rejection of the Constitution precipitated a deep crisis in the EU. Initially the political elites adopted 'a wait and see' position, arguing that the No votes were but temporary set-backs, as other countries had already ratified the Constitution. Within two days of the Dutch referendum, French President Jacques Chirac declared – following a summit with Chancellor Schroeder in Berlin – that the process of ratification had to proceed forthwith. Initially this position was supported by other countries, such as Denmark, Poland and Ireland (which declared their intention of proceeding with referendums on the Treaty irrespective of the French and Dutch rejections). This position was not based on a solid consensus, however. Dutch Prime Minister Jan-Peter Balkenende, who had campaigned for a Yes in the Netherlands, declared that a second Dutch referendum was 'out of the question' – and that the Constitution was effectively dead. The same stance – couched in more diplomatic lingo – was adopted by the British Government, which on 6 June declared that for the time being it was suspending enabling legislation for a referendum on the Constitution.

Following the British suspension, Denmark and Ireland followed suit and postponed their referendums indefinitely – a wise decision, it would seem, as all opinion polls in those countries pointed to a No. To be sure, on 10 July, a majority of the Luxembourg voters voted in support of the Treaty by a 55–45 per cent split. Luxembourg's Foreign Minister contended that his country had contributed to the healing of the 'sick' patient of Europe. But this optimistic assessment led to little more than a few sarcastic smirks on the part of the international media, or as the *Economist* (16 July 2005) put it: 'It will take more than a few plucky Luxebourgeois to defrost [the European Constitution Treaty]'.

Conclusion

What is a rebel? Of what does the rebel's No consist? Does it, for example, mean 'You've gone too far, there is a limit beyond which you may not pass'? Thus asked Albert Camus, in *L'homme révolté* (1951, 24). It might seem high-browed to quote a Nobel Laureate's treatise on existentialist philosophy in relation to something as mundane as these referendums. Yet somehow his comment seems pertinent.

This chapter has answered the question why the Dutch and French voters voted No to the European Constitution and why their counterparts in Luxembourg and Spain supported it. Having combined an account of the four referendums, with opinion polls and having contrasted the results with factors that traditionally have an impact on the outcome of referendums, we can conclude that the referendum results were shaped broadly by two factors: disquiet among the socialist voters and opposition to the EU from unskilled and low-waged employees.

There is no evidence to support the widely held belief that the referendums were verdicts on unpopular government leaders; indeed, both Chirac's and Balkenende's core supporters voted for the Constitution. Nor is there any evidence in support of the economic voting thesis and the 'honeymoon', or new government, theory. Indeed, the polls show that the moderately conservative voters supported the Treaty, while a majority of the socialist voters (supporters of, respectively, PS in France and PvdA in the Netherlands) voted No (we do not have statistical evidence from Luxembourg and Spain). This tendency – so we might speculate – could be a result of the fact that the Constitution was drafted by mainly right-leaning (conservative) governments and not by socialist governments (as was the case with the Maastricht Treaty, which was opposed by conservative voters but supported by socialist voters in France).

Among the political elites there has been much recrimination about the referendum. One widely held argument – both before and (especially) after the votes – is that referendums are ill-suited to decide big public issues. Another view is that the referendum merely performed its function as a people's veto. The German philosopher Jürgen Habermas, a supporter of the Constitution, noted in *Süddeutsche Zeitung* (2005, 2):

Referendums are a healthy, even necessary, corrective to a political elite, which through *pillarization* has abandoned the interaction between government and the governed. In so far as the voters felt that they were under-represented, it was with good reason that they opposed the non-opposed (*oppositionslose*) regime in Brussels.

10

Absentee voting: a comparative perspective

Problems with postal voting in recent elections in Australia and in the UK have attracted attention. This final chapter reviews international experiences with absentee, or postal, voting in developed capitalist democracies. In the wake of the 2004 federal election in Australia concerns were raised about the problems with postal voting in Australia. The Australian Electoral Commission recently acknowledged that there were serious problems with the distribution and production of postal voting packages especially in Queensland. This 'fiasco', led to severe criticism from Commission members (Uhlmann 2005, 48).

Whereas these concerns have been addressed in a report prepared by the law firm Minter Ellison (Australian Electoral Commission 2005), there are issues regarding absentee voting generally that have not been considered. Hitherto, the effect and implications of voting by post have been confined to ideographical case studies of single countries or states (Magleby 1987; Southwell and Burchett 2000; Banducci and Karp 2001). Yet, while such studies are of considerable merit, the failure to compare systems with one another arguably makes it likely that we will draw conclusions on the basis of an insufficient number of cases. John Stuart Mill famously noted, in *A System of Logic*, that if the findings for one country are 'not adequately compared with other instances nothing is more probable than that a wrong law will emerge instead of a right one' (Mill 1973, 917). His point remains pertinent to political science in general and in particular as regards the evaluation of democratic institutions and voting. While most other aspects of voting have been subjected to comparative scrutiny, postal voting has not.

Why postal voting?

Postal voting is the use of the postal ballot as a more or less comprehensive alternative to attendance voting. Instead of having a day on which people attend polling booths to cast their votes, voters receive a ballot paper by post and then have a period in which to return their vote by mail prior to election day. *All*-postal voting is a novelty (Hamilton 1988): while absentee voting has been available in most democracies since universal suffrage was introduced (IDEA 2004), it is only in recent years that this means of voting has been extended to the electorate at large.

Experiments with all-postal voting began in California in the late 1970s and soon spread to other states and other countries (Magleby 1987, 80). Traditionally postal votes were available only to those who could show that they had a legitimate reason, such as hospitalisation or military service, not to be in their own constituency on polling day; indeed, in Australia, postal voting was introduced for servicemen in the referendum on conscription in 1917, ostensibly because the Government considered servicemen to be positively inclined to Prime Minister Billy Hughes's bellicose foreign policy (Massicotte, Blais and Yoshinaka 2004, 133).

The picture has changed since the mid-1980s. To understand this change it is important that the extension of postal voting be seen in the context of wider political developments, especially the seemingly inexorable drop in turnout for elections and referendums (Patterson and Caldiera 1985).

Postal voting has been introduced, by and large, to reverse the trend of lessening participation rates in electoral contests. The main argument for postal voting has been that it would reduce what economists call the 'transaction costs' of polling-booth attendance (Karp and Banducci 2001). To go to the polls is, so the argument runs, an inconvenience; by allowing people to vote from home, the costs of voting would be reduced and 'turnout' rates would rise.

It has been an implicit assumption that the general extension of postal voting would be beneficial especially to low-resource groups, i.e. those socio-economic groups who, for a number of reasons, have the lowest level of electoral participation, such as the least educated, minority and ethnic groups, and low-wage earners. The League of Woman Voters, which was instrumental in getting all-postal voting introduced in Oregon, put it thus: 'Vote by Mail is convenient for all people – those with various physical challenges, those who work, those who want to study the issues and vote at home, those who don't want to be harassed by late smear campaigns' (Oregon Secretary of State 1996). This view is supported by political scientist David Magleby's survey (1987, 81), in which he remarked that 'the most common reasons advocates offer to adopt a mail ballot is that it improves participation. The impact of mail ballot elections is assumed to be especially large among persons without cars, the elderly, handicapped, or those who live at great distances from the polling place.'

While the aim of increasing turnout has been the overt reason for introducing postal voting in most jurisdictions, it is not the only one. In Australia – where there is compulsory voting for federal and state elections – postal voting has been introduced in many states for local elections to boost turnout (voting is not compulsory in these contests), but also as a part of restructuring and streamlining of the public sector. 'Universal postal voting', as an evaluation put it, 'came to Australia in the mid-1990s as part of a wider process of what has been variously been described as neo-liberal, new public management or micro-economic reforms' (Kiss 2003, 8).

Postal voting attracted reformers seeking to reduce public spending who believed that it would be cheaper to conduct all-mail elections. They were right in this. Estimates from Australia's all-postal vote for half of the members of the Constitutional Convention in 1997 suggest that the cost of the exercise was less than half of that of a ballot election – $24 million against $60 million (Massicotte, Blais and Yoshinaka 2004, 134). Generally, the 'cost of conducting all-mail elections is one third to one half of the amount required for polling place elections' (Southwell and Burchett 2000, 77).

Australia was not alone in adopting postal voting for that reason. The same cost-cutting argument was used in Oregon, where all postal local elections were introduced in the early 1980s in order to reduce voting costs. Since the mid-1980s this rationale has all but disappeared from the debate. Whatever one thinks of this reason for introducing the system, calculations have shown that voting by mail *is* considerably cheaper than ballot-voting: in Oregon the cost per ballot was US$4.33 against a mere $1.24 per postal vote (Oregon Secretary of State 1995, 4). Oregon is not the only state to have saved money from using an all-postal vote method. In New Zealand, in the country's first – and so far only – all-postal electoral contest, the electoral authorities saved an estimated US$3.6 million (Karp and Banducci 2001, 224).

The introduction of all-postal voting

Postal voting is known mostly from the USA and Australia. The western US state of Oregon has become – at least for election anoraks – almost synonymous with postal voting (Karp and Benducci 2001). In Oregon postal voting has been in use in local elections since 1981, and it was extended to special elections in 1987. In June 1993, Oregon held its first state-wide all-mail election to decide a referendum on urban renewal, and three years later a special all-mail election was held for the US Senate following the resignation of Senator Bob Packwood. The apparent success of this election led the League of Women Voters to organise a petition drive for a legislative initiative on the introduction of all-postal voting (thus using a provision in the Oregon Constitution that allows the citizens to put a bill to a referendum if 6 per cent of the citizenry sign a petition in support of this). In the subsequent referendum in 1998 on Measure 60, a majority of 67 per cent of the voters supported the proposition. Since that time, all elections in Oregon have been conducted by mail (Southwell 2004, 1).

As noted above, in 1997 half of the delegates to the Australian Constitutional Convention were elected in an all-mail ballot, while the other half were appointed (Massicotte et al. 2004, 136). Every registered voter was posted an election kit containing ballot paper and information about the process. Postal voting was established in several Australian states during the 1990s, and what makes Australia interesting in this respect is that those states have adopted the system to differing degrees, which makes it possible to draw comparative conclusions:

• Postal voting is now the legislatively prescribed system in Tasmania and South Australia.
• It is optional in Victoria (70 out of 79 councils use it) and Western Australia (though used only by a minority);
• Postal voting is available (under certain circumstances) in Queensland but unavailable in New South Wales (Russell 2004).

But whereas the introduction of postal voting in Oregon was driven by popular demand, the reverse was true in Australia (see above) where the system was introduced top–down by conservative (i.e. right of centre) state governments eager to cut costs (Kiss 2003, 6).

Other countries have also introduced postal voting. In Britain, in the local lections in England in May 2003 a total of 39 local authorities held all-postal voting elections, and in 2004, the referendum on the establishment of a regional assembly for the north east of England was carried out entirely by postal voting. The latter referendum was the first – and so far also the last – electoral contest in the UK to have been held entirely as a postal vote. In New Zealand postal ballots are now used in all municipal elections (Massicotte et al. 2004, 133). Similarly, the Compulsory Retirement Savings Scheme referendum in New Zealand in 1997 was carried out entirely by postal voting. In both these cases, the introduction of experiments with all-postal voting was a result of concerns about declining turnout among the political elite. However, unlike in Oregon, the experiments were driven from the top rather than from public demand.

The effect of postal voting

Postal voting has had many effects – some intended (e.g. higher turnout), others unintended (e.g. accusations of fraud). Fraud is the factor most commonly cited in arguments against all-postal voting. Although a councillor in Birmingham (UK) was recently found guilty of electoral fraud, there is little evidence to suggest that abuse of postal voting is widespread. A survey conducted in Oregon, for example, found that 'only 3 individuals, or .3% of all voters . . . [felt] pressured to vote a certain way. Of these three, only one indicated that he/she voted differently as a result of this pressure' (Southwell and Burchett 1997, 54). Such evidence is insufficient to prove the absence of fraud, but it does seem that the issue is generally overstated.

Yet, voting by mail has a number of other – perhaps less frequently debated – effects. If democracy is under discussion, it might be argued that traditional attendance at the polling booth is not an empty ritual: to queue up with other voters allows one to engage in political discussion, and generally to participate in an election does promote the development of citizens' democratic and civic education. Moreover, by inviting citizens 'to vote early' by postal ballot, there is a risk that they pass judgement on only part of the campaign, taking no account of political developments up to the eve of polling day. Certain critics thus 'lament the loss of camaraderie of the polling place and emphasise the importance of such socialising experience for their children' (Southwell and Burchett 1997, 53).

Such concerns have led to legal challenges in California, though they were dismissed by the courts on the grounds that postal voting led to 'greater voter participation and lower administrative costs' (Magleby 1987, 79). The main reason for the increased interest in postal voting is to counter declining turnout. Many reports on postal voting have concluded that the system does indeed lead to a higher turnout. In an evaluation of the experiments with postal voting in California in the early 1980s, it was found that turnout was higher in all but one of the eight surveyed cases (ibid.). David Magleby suggested that 'the rate of participation by voting units in the mail ballot election is highly correlated with the turnout in the municipal polling place election. Statistically the relationship is strong, with an r-squared of .93 when mail ballot participation was regressed on polling place participation' (ibid., 84). In other words, it is not postal voting itself that is responsible for a higher turnout!

With regard to second-order elections, Southwell and Burchett enthusiastically declared:

> After controlling for the nature of the race, all[-]mail elections increased registered voter turnout by 10% over the expected turnout in a traditional polling place election. These data suggest that the all[-]mail experiment succeeded in the goal of achieving higher voter participation. It appears that simply relaxing the requirement that a potential voter be physically present at the polling place on the 'first Tuesday after the first Monday' has helped certain people overcome the burden of voting . . . all[-]mail elections are an electoral panacea. (2000, 76)

This assessment is, however, based on evidence from one polity only, namely Oregon, and – as all comparative political scientists know – we must not extrapolate from a single case to others.

Figures from other polities, in fact, suggest that the tendency towards higher turnout is not uniform. The referendum on the Compulsory Retirement Savings Scheme in New Zealand did, indeed, lead to a turnout of 81 percent – thus massively higher than the meagre turnout of 27 percent in the previous referendum (on the fire service, in 1995). Yet, the turnout rates for the two subsequent referendums in New Zealand – the 1999 polls on a reform of the justice system and on parliamentary reform – were higher than in the 1995 plebiscite, despite the fact that these polls were held using the traditional system (Nohlen 2001, 11). We would have expected the opposite if it were the case that postal voting leads to an increase in turnout rate. Further, the all-postal vote in north-east England (on the proposed Regional Assembly) did not boost turnout: the proposal was rejected by 77.9 percent on a meagre 47.7 percent turnout.

These considerations may not be relevant for Australia where voting is compulsory. However, it is perhaps noteworthy that less than half of the electors voted for the Constitutional Convention in 1997, when voting was not compulsory (Massicotte et al. 2004, p. 136). To be sure, New Zealand and Britain are somewhat different as the referendums referred to above were held as pilots. It is in general true that postal voting has a positive effect on participation. However, increased turnout does not in itself prove that postal voting has lived up to its expectations. First, it is possible that the turnout stagnates among the groups whose interest postal voting is intended to stimulate. Second, it is possible that turnout has gone up simply as a result of what we might call the novelty factor; i.e. electors are likely to try something because it is new. These two possibilities will be addressed in turn.

If the rationale for postal voting is to increase the turnout rates of disadvantaged and *de facto* disenfranchised groups, it is not enough to survey the overall increase in turnout as it might be due to an increase in participation among groups that already are likely to exercise their democratic right (Oliver 1996). The question is whether increased opportunities for postal voting and, indeed, for voting by postal vote only – are likely to increase turnout among relatively excluded groups.

Whereas the early anecdotal evidence from Californian experiments in the 1980s suggested that turnout increased among all socio-economic groups (Magleby 1987), more recent assessments, using empirical evidence, suggest that the evidence is at best mixed.

The first all-postal election in Oregon did not meet the expectation of the Women's League of Voters that turnout would increase among the groups who have previously been relatively excluded from the political process. Survey data collected for the Centre for Political Studies following the Oregon special Senate election in 1993 revealed that respondents who were younger, had lower levels of education and were newly arrived in the state were less likely to vote. Moreover, voters in rural constituencies who have to travel farther to the polling station were (contrary to expectations) not more likely to vote (Traugott 1996, 6).

Based on a broader and more recent survey of all the postal-vote elections in Oregon, a study has shown that, while turnout generally goes up as a result of the introduction of all-postal voting, this generally favours the better educated, richer, white citizens. The introduction of all-postal voting thus increased participation among college graduates by 3.6 per cent, while it had no effect on those who had not undergone higher education. Similarly, turnout will drop 2–7 per cent for every 10 per cent increase in non-white voters (Karp and Banducci 2001, 233).

Karp and Banducci note in their report that voting by post 'will not mobilize groups that traditionally participate at lower rates' (ibid.). The expectation that all-postal voting increases participation among relatively excluded groups is not unequivocally supported by the evidence. Given this bias in turnout, it is perhaps not surprising that a recent study found that Republicans have an advantage when postal voting is introduced (ibid., 183).

Similar tendencies were not reported by Pippa Norris in her study of postal voting in the 2005 British general election, although she concluded that the 'initiative failed to generate much greater turnout overall and did not generate greater social equality in the voting population' (Norris 2005, 18). That parties on the Right are likely to attract votes from property owners and the middle classes is an assumption supported by data from elsewhere. In Australia, where non-resident property-based voting is part of the electoral system, all-postal voting makes it easier for those property-based citizens to vote, thereby favouring the middle-classes. Evidence that this has happened is available in the case of Victoria, where the Victorian Electoral Commission has drawn attention to the higher rate of participation achieved among non-resident voters (Kiss 1999).

However, in the City of Melbourne's 1996 post-election review it was noted that the participation rates among all categories of voters were then similar (ibid., 8). Further, in a survey study of the 1996 special Senate election in Oregon, Southwell and Burchett (1997, 56) found that the turnout rate for adults in single-parent households increased by 2.1 per cent and the rate for non-whites increased by 4.4 per cent.

Postal voting, as we have seen, was largely introduced to reverse the seemingly inexorable trend towards a lower turnout in elections. There are several empirical studies which suggest that absentee voting may have a positive impact on political interest and participation (Sparrow 2000). A report from the UK Office of the Deputy Prime Minister (ODPM) concluded its assessment of the British pilots, that 'in all but three pilots all-postal voting has produced higher turnouts than in preceding comparable elections, suggesting that for significant numbers of voters it has removed an obstacle which prevented them from voting' (ODPM Committee 2004, 15). However, the same report raised doubts, albeit in passing, about the sustainability of this tendency: was it possible that the 'turnout at all-postal elections may drop once the novelty wears off'? (ibid.).

While there is little support for this tendency in Oregon, where turnout has remained steady after the introduction of all-postal voting, there is evidence from Western Australia that turnout has tended to drop after the introduction of postal voting. Having initially seen turnouts at above 70 per cent, this participation rate had dropped to the mid-50s after only two all-postal elections.

Conclusion

Elections and referendums are typically conducted on a single day and at designated places. While this is still the norm, many jurisdictions have begun to experiment with absentee voting, i.e. elections where voters vote ahead of polling day and from places other than polling stations. Traditionally an addendum to ballot-box voting, absentee voting has become a comprehensive alternative to attendance voting. The State of Oregon has introduced wholesale postal voting – citizens vote by post in all elections and referendums. In some jurisdictions, e.g. in South

Australia and Tasmania, postal voting has been introduced for all *local* elections, but not for federal and state elections.

Postal voting gained prominence in the early 1980s when the system was favoured for cost-cutting reasons. Latterly, however, postal voting has been introduced to reverse the trend towards a lower turnout (especially among the less resourced sections of the electorate).

Postal voting has had an impact. Turnout has tended to be higher in contests that allow for postal voting. Contrary to the fears of some, this higher level of turnout does not generally decline once the novelty of postal voting wears off. While universal figures are not available, it is perhaps to be doubted that postal voting has had a positive effect on the generally low participation rates of the least educated and the marginalised citizen groups. In fact, figures from both Oregon and Australia seem to indicate that postal voting leads to higher turnout among the middle classes (a group that already participates), whereas the effect on the turnout of less resourced voters seems miniscule – if not directly negative. However, the evidence is mixed, and there are studies that have found the opposite effect, i.e. that the least resourced voters have increased participation rates. More empirical research is required to gauge the effect of this alternative to traditional voting.

Conclusion: *quo vadis* democracy?

The Speaker of the House of Commons was not in a good mood. Her gaze was stern and her expression grave when she addressed the House thus:

> The level of cynicism about Parliament, and the accompanying alienation of many of the young from the democratic process, is troubling . . . It is our responsibility, each and every one of us, to do what we can to develop and build public trust and confidence [in democracy]. (Boothroyd 2000, 1113–1114)

Ms Betty Boothroyd was right to warn Parliament against the ever-present dangers of political apathy – turnout has dropped in recent years (though it did go up marginally in 2005). However, politics is more than just voting. The idea that political involvement is nothing more than our right to choose our rulers, as proposed by John Stuart Mill and Joseph Schumpeter, is but one model of democracy – and not an unchallenged one at that.

Twentieth-century writers and politicians have argued that political participation can assume other forms, including protests, signing a petition and being involved in communal activities. If measured by the yardstick of those activities, the level of political engagement is not as low as is sometimes assumed. Contrary to the often negative assessments of the state of citizen engagement, chapter 3 of this book has shown that citizens have not become apathetic and that young people reportedly are more interested in politics as their elders.

That said, there *are* indications that traditional political engagement has declined and that the political system needs to allow for different forms of democratic participation if citizen politics is to thrive, and lest the citizens feel alienated and resort to such other (pathological) forms of political participation as terrorism.

Political decision-making, I said in the Introduction, can take the forms of talking, voting and fighting. It is only when the former two fall into

disuse that the latter comes into play. Terrorism, like war, is the continuation of politics by other means; violence, however, rarely resolves the
issues. What is needed, therefore, are ways in which the ideals of talking
and voting – sometimes in combination and sometimes alone – can be
redeveloped to ensure that we all contribute to shaping our societies. In
recent years – and not least under the influence of radical democratic
theorists – there have been many attempts to use new technologies (e-
democracy) and new institutional devices (such as postal voting) to
encourage participation. As was shown in chapters 5 and 10, such mechanisms can increase overall participation, but tend to do so by increasing turnout among the groups that are already engaged. The result is not,
therefore, a broader interest, but growing political involvement among
the already over-represented middle classes!

It might be argued, therefore, that the problem with politics is not
institutional but *social*. This would be too narrow an interpretation, for
while there are indications that class and education are strong predictors of political engagement in the USA, this is less so in the UK.
Moreover, there are indications that, by introducing the new mechanisms of participation, political inequalities might once again emerge.

What then is to be done? Perhaps nothing at all! British democracy is
not a haven of political participation, let alone a new Athens like
espoused by some radical theorists (e.g. Hannah Arendt). One might ask
whether it is even desirable that people should participate all the time.
A strong case could, indeed, be made for the view that we should be
careful not to drain the voters' civic reserves.

But no matter how we look at it, turnout in elections is too low. That
the number of people who do not participate is larger than the number
who vote in the governing party – as was the case in the general election in 2005 – is a problem that needs to be addressed. But, as argued
in chapter 6, it is not just institutional factors that are responsible for
low turnouts: another culprit could be the death of ideologies.

Politics has been defined as 'struggle'. According to German theoretician Carl Schmitt, the concept of 'the political' was based on the opposition between friend and foe (1996, 26):

> In the realm of morality the final distinctions are between good and evil,
> in aesthetics between beautiful and ugly, in economics between profitable
> and unprofitable . . . the specific distinction to which political actions and
> motives can be reduced is that between friend and enemy.

Some have argued that we are now living in a post-political era in which
all arguments are essentially technical, that the struggle has been replaced
by a technocratic vision of *evidence-based policy-making*, where ideologies

matter less than technical expertise. Ideologies have, to be sure, lost some of their potency – and this may not be altogether lamentable.

However, it is still the case that politics is about values and opinions. One prominent proponent of 'the political', namely Chantal Mouffe, has recently challenged the post-ideological consensus by making a case for a return to political struggle (2005). In Mouffe's view it is an essential human trait that we have an urge 'to belong', i.e. be part of a 'we-group', which is always defined in relation to a 'they-group'. We cannot, she argues with reference to the work of psychoanalyst Jacques Lacan, escape these we–they oppositions. However, these antagonistic feelings need not result in 'fighting', but may be transformed into talking and voting, that is, mechanisms for resolving the inevitable tensions that are part of the human condition. In her book *On the Political* (2005), Mouffe analyses how the disappearance of ideology has had the consequence that the citizenry has no one with whom to identify. This, in Mouffe's view, is one of the reasons for the rise of right-wing populist parties such as the National Front in Britain and Pauline Hanson's One Nation Party in Australia, which now present themselves as anti-establishment and hence claim to be the real alternative. Thus, by focusing on consensus, post-political politics has become a breeding ground for extreme right-wing populism.

Interestingly, though Mouffe does not make this point, the reverse was true in the 1960s when left-wing populism emerged in response to Butskellism, i.e. the post-1950 consensus between Labour and the Conservative Party. (The term *Butskellism* was invented by the *Economist* to capture the overlap between the economic policies pursued in the 1950s first by Labour's Chancellor of the Exchequer Hugh Gaitskell and then by his successor R.A. Butler. They both pursued Keynesian theories of demand-side economics (Peele 2004, 91).

Moreover, post-ideological politics – according to Mouffe – is, in fact, anything but, as perhaps evidenced by US President George W. Bush's reference to 'rogue states' and 'the axis of evil'. Interestingly, in 2004 more people in the USA voted than in the previous fifty years. Perhaps because the contest between George W. Bush and Senator John Kerry presented the voters with a stark ideological choice!

It is not only in the USA that signs of a reawakening of ideological politics have been noted. That political debate can be re-engendered is demonstrated by the referendums in the Netherlands and France in 2005, in which the perplexed political elites were suddenly faced with an electorate who did not accept the technocratic version of politics on offer in the European Constitution.

However, from the point of view of increased democratic engagement the referendums in France and the Netherlands also show the limits to the political elite's taste for citizen participation. The governors are happy to submit issues to voters when they are likely to receive an endorsement (as was shown in Spain in the referendum there). However, as the case study of the referendums in the UK showed, the political elite is not concerned primarily to re-engage citizens – and perhaps understandably so. Rather its concern is with tactical issues.

In conclusion, this book has found the following tendencies:

- While turnout has declined, more are engaged in other civic activities.
- Young people in the UK (but not in Australia) are *more* interested in politics than their elders (though less of the former vote than do the latter).
- There are no significant differences in turnout between the various groups or classes. The exception is BMI groups, who are *functionally disenfranchised*.
- Unlike in the USA, education is not markedly correlated with political activities.
- The use of mechanisms such as e-democracy and postal voting seems likely to increase turnout among white, middle-class males, but not the functionally disenfranchised groups.
- Referendums are called mainly for strategic reasons in the UK and France (those in Luxembourg, Spain and the Netherlands in 2005, however, were called because of idealistic concerns).

So where does this leave us? Where do we go from here? In a sense the answer depends on ourselves and our hopes, visions and aspirations. The debate about citizen democracy restarts afresh for each generation. Yet some arguments remain the same. Ralf Dahrendorf, a British academic and politician born in Germany, noted of the period after the Second World War:

> What we have to do above all is to maintain the flexibility of democratic institutions, which is in some way their greatest virtue; the ability of democratic institutions to implement and effect change without revolution – the ability to react to new problems in new ways – the ability to develop institutions rather than to change them all the time – the ability to keep the lines of communication open between leaders and led – and the ability to make individuals count above all. (1975, 194)

That this system will be maintained is by no means a certainty. (As was shown in chapter 2, there have been ebbs and flows of democracy, though with a tendency towards more rather than less government by the people). While the people – at least in the UK – are relatively politically engaged in general and take part in a range of political activities – voting is not always one of them. While other forms of participation are important, the lower turnout rates *do* threaten the legitimacy of government action. This is a problem that we all need to address – not by mindlessly trooping to the polling station but by engaging with the leaders and by influencing politicians to become more receptive to our views. It is *our* democracy, not that of our governors. In the word of a former Lord Chancellor, Derry Irvine:

> We should not, must not, *dare* not, be complacent about the health and future of British democracy. Unless we become a nation of engaged citizens, our democracy is not secure. (Quoted in Pattie, Seyd and Whiteley 2004, xv)

References

Alford, R. (1967) 'Class Voting in Anglo-American Systems', in S.M. Lipset and S. Rokkan (eds) *Party Systems and Voter Alignments*, New York, Free Press.

Almond, Gabriel A. (1996) 'Political Science: The History of the Discipline', in R.E. Goodin and Hand-Dieter Klingemann (eds) *A New Handbook of Political Science*, Oxford, Oxford University Press.

Almond, Gabriel and Verba, Sydney (1963) *The Civic Culture*, Princeton, NJ, Princeton University Press.

Amery, L.S. (1964) *Thoughts on the Constitution*, Oxford, Oxford University Press.

Anderson, R. (1962) 'Adoption and Operation of Initiative and Referendum in Oregon', unpublished Ph.D thesis, University of Minnesota.

Andeweg, R.B. and Irwin, G.A. (2005) *Governance and Politics in the Netherlands*, 2nd edn, Houndmills, Middlesex, Palgrave.

Aquinas, Thomas de (2002) *Political Writings*, ed. R.W. Dyson, London, Blackfriars.

Arendt, H. (1958) *The Human Condition*, Chicago, University of Chicago Press.

Arendt, H. (1963) *On Revolution*, London, Penguin.

Arendt, H. (1983) *Between Past and Future*, New York, Penguin.

Arendt, H. (1994) *Essays in Understanding 1930–1954: Formation, Exile, and Totalitarianism*, ed. Jerome Kohn, New York, Schocken Books.

Arendt, H. (2000) 'What Remains? Language Remains: A Conversation with Günter Gaus', in *The Portable Hannah Arendt*, ed. Peter Baehr, London, Penguin.

Aristotle (1965) 'On the Art of Poetry', in *Aristotle, Horace, Longinus: Classical Literary Criticism*, ed. T.S. Dorsch, London, Penguin.

Aristotle (1984) *The Athenian Constitution*, London, Penguin.

Aristotle (1988) *The Politics*, Cambridge, Cambridge University Press.

Aristotle (1991) *The Art of Rhetoric*, London, Penguin.

Aristotle (2004) *The Nicomachean Ethics*, London, Penguin.

Aron, R. (1994) *In Defence of Political Reason*, Lanham, MD, Rowman & Littlefield.

Arterton, F.C. (1987) *Teledemocracy: Can Technology Protect Democracy?*, Newbury Park, CA, Sage.

Augustine (1984) *The City of God*, Penguin, London.

Australian Defence Review (2000) *Our Future Defence Force*, Canberra, Department of Defence.

Australian Electoral Commission (2005) www.aec.gov.au.

Bagehot, Walter (2001 [1867]) *The English Constitution*, Oxford, Oxford University Press.

Banducci, S.A. and Karp, J. (2000) 'Going Postal: How All-Mail Elections Influence Turnout', *Political Behaviour*, Vol. 22, No. 3.

Banducci, S.A. and Karp, J. (2001) 'Absentee Voting, Participation, and Mobilization', *American Politics Research*, Vol. 29, No. 2.

Barber, B. (1984) *Strong Democracy: Participatory Democracy for a New Age*, Berkeley, University of California Press.

Barns, Greg (2005) *Selling the Australian Government: Politics and Propaganda from Whitlam to Howard*, Sydney, University of New South Wales Press.

Barthes, R. (2000) *Mythologies*, London, Vintage.

Batchelor, Anthony (2005) 'Democratic Triumph or Flawed Reform? The Growth of Direct Democracy in the UK since 1970', *Politics Review*, Vol. 15, No. 1.

Bean, C. (2005) 'Young People's Voting Patterns', paper presented at the Youth Electoral Study Workshop, Old Parliament House, Canberra, June.

Beer, S.H. (1966) 'The British Legislature and the Problem of Mobilizing Consent', in E. Frank (ed.) *Lawmakers in a Changing World*, Englewood Cliffs, NJ, Prentice-Hall.

Becker, T. and Scarce, R. (1984) 'Teledemocracy Emergent: The State of the Art and Science', paper presenteded at the APSA Annual Meeting, Washington, DC.

Birch, A.H. (1964) *Representative and Responsible Government: An Essay on the British Constitution*, London, Allen & Unwin.

Bjørklund, T. (1982) 'The Demand for a Referendum: When Does it Arise and When Does it Succeed?', *Scandinavian Political Studies*, Vol. 5, No. 3.

Black, Joan S. (1982) 'Opinion Leaders: Is Anyone Following?', *Public Opinion Quarterly*, Vol. 46, No. 2.

Blair, T. (1996) 'Democracy's Second Age', *Economist*, 14 September.

Blais, A. and Carty, K. (1990) 'Does Proportional Representation Foster Voter Turnout?', *Journal of Political Research*, Vol. 18, No. 2.

Blais, André (2000) *To Vote or Not to Vote: The Merits and Limits of Rational Choice Theory*, Pittsburg, PA, University of Pittsburg Press.

Bobbio, N. (1995) *Il futuro della democrazia*, Turin, Einaudi.

Bogdanor, V.B. (ed.) (1991) *The Blackwell Encyclopaedia of Political Science*, Oxford, Blackwell.

Bogdanor, V.B. (1994) 'Western Europe', in David Butler and Austin Ranney (eds) *Referendums Around the World: The Growing Use of Direct Democracy*, London, Macmillan.

Bogdanor, V.B. (1996) *Politics and the Constitution: Essays in British Government*, Aldershot, Dartmouth Publishing.

Boothroyd, B. (2000) *The House of Commons Official Report*, 26 July, cols 1113–1114, London, Stationery Office.

Bowler, S. and Donovan, T. (1998) *Demanding Choices*, Ann Arbor, University of Michigan Press.

Bryce, J. (1921) *Modern Democracies*, London, Macmillan.

Burke, E. (1902) 'Speech to the Electors in Bristol', in *The Works of the Right Honourable Edmund Burke*, Vol. 1, London, Bohn's Library.

Burke, E. (1998) 'A Philosophical Enquiry into the Sublime and the Beautiful', in *A Philosophical Enquiry into the Origin of Our Ideas of the Sublime and the Beautiful; and Other Pre-Revolutionary Writings*, ed. D. Womersley, London, Penguin.

Butler, D. (1960) 'The Paradox of Party Difference', *American Behaviouralist*, Vol. 4, No. 4.

Butler, D. and Kitzinger, U. (1975) *The 1975 Referendum*, London, Macmillan.

Butler, D. and Ranney, A. (1978) *Referendums: A Survey of Practice and Theory*, Washington, DC, American Enterprise Institute.

Butler, D. and Stokes, D. (1974) *Political Change in Britain*, London, Macmillan.

Camus, Albert (1951) *L'homme révolté*, Paris, Edition Gallimard.

Carson, L. (1999) 'Policy Juries: A Case Study', in L. Shilneva (ed.) *Questions of Life – Social Work and Social Pedagogics: Conclusions, Experience and Practice*, Riga, Latvia, Attistiba Higher School of Social Work and Social Pedagogics.

Carson, L. (2001) 'Stimulating the Voice of the Voiceless', *Third Sector Review*, Vol. 7, No. 2.

Carson, L. (2004) 'Reflections from Down Under on the Biggest Deliberation in History', *Group Facilitation: A Research and Applications Journal*, Special Issue: 'Listening to the City', Vol. 6, spring.

Carter, A. (1986) 'Civil Disobedience', in David Miller (ed.) *The Blackwell Encyclopaedia of Political Thought*, Oxford, Blackwell.

Cicero, Marcus Tullius (1998) *The Republic: The Laws*, ed. Jonathan Powell, Oxford, Oxford University Press.

Clarke, Harold D., Sanders, David, Stewart, Marianne C. and Whiteley, Paul (2005) *Political Choice in Britain*, Oxford, Oxford University Press.

Coleman, S. and Gøtze, J. (2004) *Bowling Together: Online Public Engagement in Policy Deliberation*, London, Hansard Society.

Cooper, Duane A. (2004) 'Spatial Analysis of Cumulative Voting with Modeling for Dynamical System Simulation', in G.S. Ladde, N.G. Medhin and M. Sambandham (eds) *Proceedings of Dynamic Systems and Applications*, Vol. 4, Atlanta, GA, Dynamic Publishers.

Coote, A. and Lenaghan, J. (1997) *Citizens' Juries: From Theory to Practice*, London, IPPR.

Cosgrove, Richard (1981) *Albert Venn Dicey: Victorian Jurist*, London, Macmillan.

Crenshaw, Martha (1990) 'Questions to Be Answered, Research to Be Done, Knowledge to Be Applied', in Walter Reich (ed.) *Origins of Terrorism: Psychologies, Ideologies, Theologies, States of Mind*, Cambridge, Cambridge University Press.

Crick, B. (1986) *In Defence of Politics*, London, Penguin.

Cronin, T. (1989) *Direct Democracy: The Politics of Initiative, Referendum and Recall*, Cambridge, MA, Harvard University Press.

Dahl, Robert A. (1989) *Democracy and its Critics*, New Haven, CT, Yale University Press.

Dahrendorf, Ralf (1975) 'Excepts from Remarks on the Ungovernability Study', in

M. Crozier, S.P. Huntington and J. Watanuki (eds) *The Crisis of Democracy*, New York, New York University Press.

Dalton, Russell (1998) *Citizen Politics*, Chatham, NJ, Chatham House Publishers.

Dalton, Russell (2002) *Citizen Politics: Public Opinion and Political Parties in Advanced Industrial Democracies*, Washington, DC, Congressional Quarterly Press.

Dante Alighieri (1979) *De monarchia*, Milan, Ricciardi.

Dayell, T. (2005) 'Reflections on Leaving Parliament', *Political Quarterly*, Vol. 76, No. 3.

Dicey, A.V. (1982) *An Introduction to the Study of the Law of the Constitution*, Indianapolis, IN, Liberty Fund.

Dicey, A.V. (1890) 'Ought the Referendum to Be Introduced into England?', *Contemporary Review*, Vol. 57.

Dostoevsky, F.M. (2000) *Devils: The Possessed*, Oxford, Oxford University Press.

Downs, Anthony (1957) *An Economic Theory of Democracy*, New York, Harper.

Dumond, P. and Poirier, P. (2004) 'Luxembourg', *European Journal of Political Research*, Vol. 43, No. 4.

Dumont, P. and de Winter, L. (2003) 'Luxembourg: A Case for More "Direct" Delegation and Accountability', in K. Strøm, W.C. Müller and T. Bergman (eds) *Delegation and Accountability in Parliamentary Democracies*, Oxford, Oxford University Press.

Dunkerley, D. and Glasner, P. (1998) 'Empowering the Public? Citizens' Juries and the New Genetic Technologies', *Critical Public Health*, Vol. 8, No. 3.

Duverger, Maurice (1980) *Modern Democracies*, New York, Henry Holt & Co.

ICPSR (2003) *Dutch Parliamentary Election Study*, Ann Arbor, MI: Inter-University Consortium for Political and Social Research.

Duverger, Maurice (1992) *Les partis politiques*, Paris, Seuil.

Electoral Commission (2002a) *Reinvigorating Local Democracy? Mayoral Referendums in 2001*, London, Electoral Commission.

Electoral Commission (2002b) *Voter Engagement and Young People*, online: www.electoralcommission.gov.uk/files/dms/Researcharchive-Youngpeople_6846-6356_E_N_S_W.pdf (accessed 3 March 2006).

Electoral Commission (2002c) *Voter Engagement Among Black and Minority Ethnic Communities*, online: www.electoralcommission.org.uk/files/dms/Ethnicfinalreport_11586–6190_E_N_S_W.pdf (accessed 4 March 2006).

Electoral Commission (2004) *The 2004 European Parliamentary Elections in the United Kingdom*, London, Electoral Commission.

Emden, Cecil (1962) *The People and the Constitution*, Oxford, Oxford University Press.

Encarnación, Omar G. (2001–2002) 'After Franco: Lessons in Democratization', *World Policy Journal*, Vol. 18, No. 4.

English, R. (2003) *The United States Congress*, Manchester, Manchester University Press.

Esposito, John L. (2002) *Unholy War: Terror in the Name of Islam*, Oxford, Oxford University Press.

European Social Survey (2002) www.europeansocialsurvey.org

Euripedes (1958) *Suppliant Women*, Chicago, University of Chicago Press.

Fanon, F. (1961) *The Wretched of the Earth*, New York, Grove Press.

Fenno, Richard E., Jr (1990) *Watching Politicians: Essays on Participant Observation*, Berkeley, CA, IGS Press.

Filmer, R. (1949 [1680]) *Patriarcha and Other Political Works*, ed. Peter Laslett, Oxford, Blackwell.

Finer, S.E. (1998) *The History of Government*, 3 vols, Oxford, Oxford University Press.

Finley, M.I. (1983) *Politics in the Ancient World*, Cambridge, Cambridge University Press.

Friedenberg, R.V. (1999) 'A Prehistory of Media Consulting for Political Campaigns', in D.D. Perlmutter (ed.) *The Manship School Guide to Political Communication*, Baton Rouge, Louisiana State University Press.

Fukuyama, F. (1989) 'The End of History', *National Interest*, Vol. 16, summer.

Gadamer, Hans-Georg (2004) *Truth and Method*, London, Continuum.

Gallagher, Michael and Vincenzo Uleri, Pier (eds) (1996) *The Referendum Experience in Europe*, London, Macmillan.

Gay, Oonagh, Winetrobe, Berry K. and Wood, Edward (1997) *The Greater London Authority (Referendum) Bill: Bill 61 of 1997–1998*, House of Commons Library, Research Paper No. 97/114.

Geertsema, D. (1987) *Het Referendum: Bijl aan de wortels van de democratie*, De Haan, Houlten.

Geertz, Clifford (1973) *The Interpretation of Cultures*, New York, Basic Books.

Gilhuis, P.C. (1981) *Het Referendum: Een rechtsvergelijkende studie*, Hague, Alphen aan den Rijn

Goethe, J.W. von (1958) *Faust*, Parts 1 and 2, Munich, Wilhelm Goldmann.

Goldthorpe, John (1980) *Social Mobility and Class Structure in Modern Britain*, Oxford, Oxford University Press.

Goodin, Robert and Klingemann, Hans-Dieter (eds) (2006) *The Oxford Handbook of Political Science*, Oxford, Oxford University Press.

Gould, P. (1998) *The Unfinished Revolution: How Modernisers Saved the Labour Party*, London, Little Brown & Co.

Gurr, T.R. (1970) *Why Men Rebel*, Princeton, NJ, Princeton University Press.

Habermas, Jürgen (2005) 'Europa ist uns über die Köpfe hinweggerollt', *Süddeutsche Zeitung*, 6 June.

Hamilton, A., Madison, J. and Jay, J. (1996) *The Federalist Papers*, London, Everyman.

Hamilton, R. (1988) 'American All-Mail Balloting: A Decade's Experience', *Public Administration Review*, Vol. 48, No. 4.

Hampsher-Monk, I. (1976) 'The Political Theory of the Levellers', *Political Studies*, Vol. 24. No. 4.

Hansard Society (1992) *Making the Law: Report of the Hansard Society on the Legislative Process*, London, Hansard.

Hansen, M. (1976) 'How Many Athenians Attended the Ecclesia', *Greek, Roman and Byzantine Studies*, Vol. 17, No. 1.

Harmsen, Robert (2005) *The Dutch Referendum on the Ratification of the European Constitutional Treaty*, EPERN Referendum Briefing Paper No.13.

Heath, Anthony, Curtice, John and Jowell, Roger (1985) *How Britain Votes*, Oxford, Oxford University Press.

Hegel, G.W.F. (1988) *Introduction to the Philosophy of History*, trans. Leo Rauch, Indianapolis, IN, Hackett.

Held, D. (1996) *Models of Democracy*, 2nd edn, Stanford, CA, Stanford University Press.

Henn, M., Weinstein, M. and Wring, D. (2002) 'A Generation Apart? Youth and Political Participation in Britain', *British Journal of Politics and International Relations*, Vol. 4, No. 2.

Hirschman, A. (1970) *Exit, Voice, and Loyalty*, Cambridge, MA, Harvard University Press.

House of Commons Debates, www.parliament.uk

Hume, David (1985) 'That Politics May Be Reduced to a Science', in *Essays: Moral, Political and Literary*, Indianapolis, IN, Liberty Fund.

Huntington, S.P. (1996) *The Clash of Civilizations and the Remaking of World Order*, New York, Simon & Schuster.

Inglehart, Ronald (1977) *The Silent Revolution*, Princeton, NJ, Princeton University Press.

Inglehart, R. (1997) *Modernization and Post-Modernization: Cultural, Economic and Political Change in 43 Countries*, Princeton, NJ, Princeton University Press.

International Institute for Democratic and Electoral Assistance (IDEA) (2004) *Postal Voting and Voting on the Internet*, online: www.idea.int/vt/postal_voting_internet_voting.cfm (accessed 27 May 2005).

IPSOS (2005) www.ipsos.fr/CanalIpsos/articles/1545.asp.

James, William (1948 [1911]) *Some Problems of Philosophy*, New York, Longman, Green & Co.

Jehne, M. (1995) *Demokratie in Rom: Die Rolle des Volkes in der Politik der späten römerischen Republik*, Stuttgart, Steiner.

Johnson, D.W. (2001) *No Place for Amateurs: How Political Consultants Are Reshaping American Democracy*, New York, Routledge.

Jones, Bill (2004) *Dictionary of British Politics*, Manchester, Manchester University Press.

Josephus (1970) *The Jewish War*, London, Penguin.

Joyce, Peter (2002) *The Politics of Protest: Extra-Parliamentary Politics in Britain since 1970*, Houndmills, Palgrave.

Katz, Richard (1997) *Democracy and Elections*, Oxford, Oxford University Press.

Kavanagh, Dennis (1996) *British Politics: Continuities and Change*, Oxford, Oxford University Press.

Key, V.O. (1966) *The Responsible Electorate*, Cambridge, MA, Belknap Press.

Kiss, R. (1999) 'It's in the Mail', in *The Pros and Cons of Postal Voting: Papers from the VLGA Forum on Universal Postal Voting, 18 June 1999*, Melbourne, Victorian Local Governance Association.

Kiss, R. (2003) 'Postal Voting for Australian Local Government: Democracy or

Conspiracy?', paper presented at the ECPR Conference, Marburg, Germany, 18–22 September.

Kojève, A. (1968) *Introduction à la lecture de Hegel*, Paris, Gallimard.

Kretzman, N., Kenny, A., Pinborg, J. and Stump, E. (1988) *The Cambridge History of Later Medieval Philosophy: From the Rediscovery of Aristotle to the Disintegration of Scholasticism*, Cambridge, Cambridge University Press.

Kristeva, J. (2001) *Hannah Arendt*, New York, Columbia University Press.

Kuhn, Thomas S. (1962) *The Structure of Scientific Revolutions*, Chicago, University of Chicago Press.

Laakso, M. and Taagapera, R. (1979) ' Effective Number of Parties: A Measure with Application to West Europe', *Comparative Political Studies*, Vol. 12, No. 1.

Labévière, Richard (1999) *Les dollars de la terreur: les états-unis et les islamistes*, Paris, Grasset.

Lake, C. (1989) 'Political Consultants: Opening Up a New System of Political Power', *Political Science and Politics*, No. 2.

Lazarsfeld, Paul F., Berelson, B. and Gaudet, Hazel (1988) *The People's Choice*, New York, Columbia University Press.

Lazarsfeld, Paul F. and Katz, Elihu (1955) *Personal Influence: The Part Played by People in the Flow of Mass Communications*, New York, Free Press.

LeDuc, L. (2003) *The Politics of Direct Democracy: Referendums in Global Perspective*, Toronto, Broadview Press.

Lee, E. (1986) 'Can Voters Be Trusted? The Local Government Referendum and Tax Reform', *Public Administration*, Vol. 66, No. 2.

Lees-Marshment, J. (2001) *The Political Marketing Revolution. Transforming the Government of the UK*, Manchester, Manchester University Press.

Lees-Marshment, J. (2004) *Political Marketing and British Political Parties*, Manchester, Manchester University Press.

Lees-Marshment, J. and Quayle, S. (2001) 'Empowering the Members or Marketing the Party? The Conservative Reforms of 1998', *Political Quarterly*, Vol. 72, No. 2.

Levine, P., Fung, A. and Gastil, J. (2005) 'Future Directions for Public Deliberation', *Journal of Public Deliberation*, Vol. 1, No. 1.

Lewis-Beck, M.S. (1993) *Regression Analysis: International Handbook of Quantitative Applications*, London, Sage.

Lewis-Beck, M.S. and Rice, T. (1990) *Forecasting Elections*, Washington, DC, CQ Press.

Lijphart, A. (1999) *Patterns of Democracy*, New Haven, CT, Yale University Press.

Lijphart, A. (1984) *Democracies: Patterns of Majoritarian and Consensus Government in Twenty-One Countries*, New Haven, CT, and London, Yale University Press.

Lipset, S.M. and Rokkan, S. (1967) 'Cleavage Structures, Party Systems, and Voter Alignments: An Introduction', in S.M. Lipset and S. Rokkan (eds) *Party Systems and Voter Alignments*, New York, Free Press.

Locke, John (1988) *Two Treatises of Government*, Cambridge, Cambridge University Press.

Lucardie, P. and Voerman, G. (2004) 'The Netherlands', *European Journal of Political Research*, Vol. 43, No. 4.

McAllister, I. (2001) 'Explaining Turnout in the 2001 British General Election', *Representation*, Vol. 38, No. 3.

McClelland, J.S. (1996) *A History of Western Political Thought*, London, Routledge.

McCormick, John (2001) 'Controlling Elites with Ferocious Populism', *American Political Science Review*, Vol. 95, No. 2.

McGarry, John and O'Leary, Brendan (1995) *Interpreting Northern Ireland*, Oxford, Blackwell.

Machiavelli, Niccoló (1965) *Discourses on the First Decade of Titus Livius*, in *Machiavelli: The Chief Works*, ed. Allan Gilbert, Vol. 1, Durham, NC, Duke University Press.

Machiavelli, Niccoló (1994) *Selected Political Writings: The Prince, Selections from the Discourses, and Letter to Vettori*, ed. David Wooton, Indianapolis, IN, Hackett.

Machiavelli, Niccoló (1998), *Il principe*, Roma, Grandi Tascabili Economici.

McKelvey, R.D. (1976) 'Intransitivities in Multidimensional Voting Models and Some Implications for Agenda Control', *Journal of Economic Theory*, Vol. 18, No. 1.

McLaverty, P. (2002) 'Is Public Participation a Good Thing?', in P. McLaverty (ed.) *Public Participation and Innovations in Community Governance*, Aldershot, Ashgate.

Macpherson, C.B. (1962) *The Political Theory of Possessive Individualism: Hobbes to Locke*, Oxford, Oxford University Press.

Macpherson, C.B. (1984) *The Life and Times of Liberal Democracy*, Oxford, Oxford University Press.

Magleby, D. (1984) *Direct Legislation. Voting on Ballot Propositions in the United States*, Baltimore, MD, Johns Hopkins University Press.

Magleby, D. (1987) 'Participation in Mail Ballot Elections', *Western Political Quarterly*, Vol. 40, No. 1.

Mailer, Norman (2003) *Why Are We at War?*, New York, Random House.

Mair, P. and Van Biezen, I. (2001) 'Party Members in 20 European Democracies 1980–2000', *Party Politics*, Vol. 7, No. 1.

Marsilius of Padua (2005) *The Defender of the Peace*, Cambridge, Cambridge University Press.

Marx, K. and Engels, F. (1985) *The Communist Manifesto*, London, Penguin.

Massicotte, L., Blais, A. and Yoshinaka, A. (2004) *Establishing the Rules of the Game: Election Laws in Democracies*, Toronto, University of Toronto Press.

May, Erskine (1997) *Parliamentary Practice*, 22nd edn, London, Butterworths.

Michels, Robert (1911) *Zur Soziologie des Parteiwesens in der modernen Demokratie: Untersuchungen über die oligarchischen Tendenzen des Gruppenlebens*, Leipzig, Klinkhardt.

Mill, J.S. (1973) 'A System of Logic', in *The Collected Works of John Stuart Mill*, ed. R.M. Robson, Vol. 7, Toronto, University of Toronto Press.

Mill, J.S. (1991) *On Liberty and Other Essays*, ed. John Gray, Oxford, Oxford University Press.

Millar, F. (2002) *The Crowd in Rome in the Late Republic*, Ann Arbor, University of Michigan Press.

Mills, C. Wright (2002 [1959]) *The Sociological Imagination*, Oxford, Oxford University Press.

Möckli, S. (1994) *Direkte Demokratie: ein internationaler Vergleich*, Stuttgart, Haupt.

Modernisation Committee (1997–1998) *First Report of the 1997–1998 Session: The Legislative Process*, HC 224–I, London, Stationery Office.

Modernisation Committee (2001–2002) *First and Second Reports of the 2001–2002 Session: Modernisation of the House of Commons: A Reform Programme* (HC 224–I and HC 1168–I), London, Stationery Office.

Modernisation Committee (2001–2002) *Carry Over of Public Bills, House of Commons*, London, Stationery Office.

Montesquieu, C.S. de (1989) *The Spirit of the Laws*, Cambridge, Cambridge University Press.

Moore, T. and Maddox, G. (1995) 'Rights, Jurisdiction and Responsible Government: The Spectre of Capital Television', *Journal of Commonwealth and Comparative Studies*, Vol. 33, No. 3.

Morel, L. (1992) 'Party Attitudes towards Referendums in Western Europe', *West European Politics*, Vol. 16, No. 3.

Morel, L. (1996) 'France: Towards a Less Controversial Use of the Referendum', in P.V. Uleri and M. Gallagher (eds) *The Referendum Experience in Europe*, London, Macmillan.

Morel, L. (2001) 'The Rise of Government Initiated Referendums in Consolidated Democracies', in M. Mendelssohn and A. Parkin (eds) *Referendum Democracy: Citizens, Elites and Deliberations in Referendum Campaigns*, London, Palgrave.

Morel, L. (2005) 'Le choix du référendum: leçons françaises: l'émergence d'un référendum politiquement obligatoire', paper presented at the ECPR General Conference, Budapest, 8–10 September.

Morris, D. (2003) 'The Future of Political Campaigning: The American Example', *Journal of Public Affairs*, Vol. 1, No. 3.

Mouffe, C. (2005) *On the Political*, London, Routledge.

Munro, Edwin B. (1912) *The Initiative, the Referendum and the Recall*, New York, Appleton.

Nie, N.H., Yerba, S. and Petrovik, J.R. (2002) *The Changing American Voter*, New York, Replica Books.

Nietzsche, Friedrich (1995) *The Complete Works of Friedrich Nietzsche*, Vol. 11: *Unpublished Writings from the Period of Unfashionable Observations*, trans. R. Gray, Stanford, CA, Stanford University Press.

Nohlen, D. (2001) *Elections in Asia and the Pacific*, Vol. 2: *South-East Asia, East Asia and the South Pacific*, Oxford, Oxford University Press.

Nohlen, D., Grotz, F., Krennerich, M. and Thibaut, B. (2000) *Electoral Systems in Independent Countries*, Washington, DC, IFES.

Norris, Pippa (1997) *Electoral Change since 1945*, Oxford, Blackwell.

Norris, Pippa (ed.) (1999) *Critical Citizens: Global Support for Democratic Government*, Oxford, Oxford University Press.

Norris, Pippa (2001) Digital Divide: Civic Engagement, Information Poverty and the Internet Worldwide, Cambridge, Cambridge University Press.

Norris, Pippa (2004) 'Will New Technology Boost Turnout?', in Norbert Kersting and Harald Baldersheim (eds) *Electronic Voting and Democracy*, London, Palgrave.

Norris, Pippa (2005) 'Rearranging the Deckchairs on the Titanic? The Impact of Postal Voting on Demand in Britain', paper prepared at the APSA Annual Meeting, Washington, DC.

Norton, Philip (2000) 'Reforming Parliament in the United Kingdom: The Report of the Commission to Strengthen Parliament', *Journal of Legislative Studies*, Vol. 6, No. 3.

Oakeshott, M. (1991) *Rationalism in Politics and Other Essays*, Indianapolis, IN, Liberty Fund.

ODPM, Housing, Planning, Local Government and the Regions Committee (2004) *Seventh Report of the 2003–2004 Session: Postal Voting* (HC 400–1), London, Stationery Office.

Oliver, Eric (1996) 'The Effects of Eligibility Restrictions and Party Activity on Absentee Voting', *American Journal of Political Science*, Vol. 4, No. 4.

ONS (1995) *Social Trends*, London, Office of National Statistics.

Oregon, Secretary of State (1995) *Oregon's Special Senate Election*, November 11.

Oregon, Secretary of State (1998) *Measure 60 Proposed by Initiative Petition to Be voted on at the General Election*, November 3, 1998.

Ortega y Gasset, J. (1937) *La rebelión de las masas*, Madrid, Austral.

Page, E.C. (1990) 'British Political Science and Comparative Politics', *Political Studies*, Vol. 38, No. 2.

Page, E.C. (2001) *Governing by Numbers: Delegated Legislation and Everyday Policy-Making*, Oxford, Portland.

Palmer, A. (1998) 'Now New Labour Backs what the Tabloid Savages', *Daily Telegraph*, 3 May.

Parlianet (2004) www.parlianet.com/background/process_ns.asp (accessed 1 December 2005).

Pateman, C. (1970) *Participation and Democratic Theory*, Cambridge, Cambridge University Press.

Patterson, Samuel C. and Caldiera, Gregory (1985) 'Mailing the Vote: Correlates and Consequences of Absentee Voting', in *American Journal of Political Science*, Vol. 29, No. 4.

Pattie, C., Seyd, P., and Whiteley, P. (2004) *Citizenship in Britain: Values, Participation and Democracy*, Cambridge, Cambridge University Press.

Pimlott, Ben and Rao, Nirmala (2002) *Governing London*, Oxford, Oxford University Press.

Peele, G. (2004) *Governing the UK*, 4th edn, Oxford, Blackwell.

Plato (1997) *Plato: Complete Works*, ed. John M. Cooper, Indianapolis, IN, Hackett.

Polsby, Nelson W. (1990) 'Parliaments', in Philip Norton (ed.) *Legislatures*, Oxford, Oxford University Press.

Polsby, Nelson W. (1998) 'Social Science and Scientific Change: A Note on Thomas S. Kuhn's Contribution', *Annual Review of Political Science*, Vol. 1.

Popper, Karl R. (1957) *The Poverty of Historicism*, London, Routledge.

Power Inquiry (2006) www.powerinquiry.org (accessed 11 May 2006).

Pulzer, P. (1967) *Political Representation and Elections in Britain*, London, Allen & Unwin.

Qvortrup, M. (1999) 'A.V. Dicey: The Referendum as the People's Veto', *History of Political Thought*, Vol. 20, No. 3.

Qvortrup, M. (2003) *The Political Philosophy of Jean-Jacques Rousseau: The Impossibility of Reason*, Manchester, Manchester University Press.

Qvortrup, M. (2004) 'In Search of Lost Time: S.E. Finer, History and the Science of Government', *European Journal of Political Research*, Vol. 43, No. 1.

Qvortrup, M. (2005) *Absentee Voting in Comparative Perspective*, submission to the Joint Committee on Electoral Matters, Australian Federal Parliament, www.aph.gov.au/house.

Rasch, Bjørn Erik (1995) 'Parliamentary Voting Procedures', in H. Döring (ed.) *Parliaments and Majority Rule in Western Europe*, Franktfurt and New York, Campus Verlag and St. Martin's Press.

Rasch, Bjørn Erik (2004) *Kampen om Regjeringsmakten: Norsk parlamentarisme i europeisk Perspektiv*, Oslo, Fakbokforlaget.

Rawls, John (1971) *A Theory of Justice*, Oxford, Oxford University Press.

Roberts J.M. (1980) *History of the World*, London, Penguin.

Rouke, J., Hiskes, R. and Zirakzadeh, E.C. (1992) *Direct Democracy and International Politics: Deciding International Issues through Referendums*, Boulder, CO, Lynne Rienner.

Rousseau, Jean-Jacques (1964) 'Discours sur l'origine et les fondements de l'inegalité parmi des hommes', in *Jean-Jacques Rousseau: Oeuvres complétes*, Paris, Gallimard.

Rousseau, Jean-Jacques (1972) *The Social Contract*, London, Dent.

Russell, B. (2004) 'Discussion Paper Prepared for the Local Government Association of South Australia', online: www.lga.sa.gov (accessed 17 September 2005).

Saggar, S. (2000) *Race and Representation*, Manchester, Manchester University Press.

Sampson, Anthony (2004) *Who Runs This Place? The Anatomy of Britain in the 21st Century*, London, John Murray.

Sanders, D. (1991) 'Government Popularity and the Next Election', in *Political Quarterly*, Vol. 62, No. 2.

Sanders, D., Clarke, H., Stewart, M. and Whiteley, P. (2005) *The 2005 General Election in Great Britain: Report to the Electoral Commission*, London, Electoral Commission.

Sartori, G. (1976) *Parties and Party Systems*, Cambridge, Cambridge University Press.

Schmitt, C. (1996) *The Concept of the Political*, Chicago, University of Chicago Press.

Schofield, N. (1978) 'Instability of Simple Dynamic Games', *Review of Economic Studies*, Vol. 45, No. 3.

Schumpeter, Josef A. (1951) *Capitalism, Socialism, and Democracy*, 2nd edn, New York, Harper & Row.

Shell, D. (1999) 'To Revise and to Deliberate: The British House of Lords', in S.C. Patterson and A. Mughan (eds) *Senates: Bicameralism in the Contemporary World*, Columbus, Ohio State University Press.

Shepsle, Kenneth A. and Bonchek, Mark S. (1997) *Analysing Politics: Rationality, Behaviour and Institutions*, London, Norton & Co.

Shi, Tianjian (1997) *Participation in Beijing*, Boston, MA, Harvard University Press.

Smelser, N. (1962) *The Theory of Collective Behaviour*, New York, Simon & Schuster.

Smith, Adam (2002) *The Theory of Moral Sentiments*, ed. Knud Haakonsen, Cambridge, Cambridge University Press.

Smith, G. and Wales, C. (2000) 'Citizen Juries and Deliberative Democracy', *Political Studies*, Vol. 48, No. 1.

Sorel, G. (1950) *Reflections on Violence*, New York, Collier.

Southwell, P.L. (2004) 'Five Years Later: A Re-Assessment of Oregon's Vote-by-Mail Electoral Process', *PS: Political Science and Politics*, Vol. 38, No.1.

Southwell, P.L. and Burchett, J.I. (1997) 'Survey of Vote-by-Mail Senate Election in the State of Oregon', *PS: Political Science and Politics*, Vol. 30. No 1.

Southwell, P.L. and Burchett, J.I. (2000) 'The Effect of All-Mail Elections on Voter Turnout', *American Politics Quarterly*, Vol. 28, No. 1.

Sparrow, A. (2000) 'Voting by Post Boosts Turnout', *Daily Telegraph*, 12 May.

Stonecash, J.M. (2003) *Political Polling: Strategic Information in Campaigns*, Lanham, MD, Rowman & Littlefield.

Szczerbiak, A. and Taggart, P. (2004) 'Conclusion: Towards a Model of (European) Referendums', *West European Politics*, Vol. 27, No. 4.

Taylor, L.R. (1966) *Roman Voting Assemblies*, Ann Arbor, University of Michigan Press.

Thucydides (1951) *The Peloponnesian War*, New York, Modern Library.

Thurber, J.A. (1998) 'The Study of Campaign Consultants: A Subfield in Search of Theory', *PS: Political Science and Politics*, Vol. 31, No. 2.

Tocqueville, A. de (1988) *De la démocratie en Amérique*, Vol. 1, Paris, Edition Folio.

Traugott, Michael (1996) *Report on the Characteristics of the Oregon Electorate Participating in the Special Election for the US Senate*, Ann Arbor, MI, Institute for Social Research.

Tsebelis, George (1994) 'The Power of the European Parliament as a Conditional Agenda Setter', *American Political Science Review*, Vol. 88, No. 1.

Tsebelis, G. and Money, J. (1998) *Bicameralism*, Cambridge, Cambridge University Press.

Uhlmann, Chris (2005) 'Polls Apart', *About the House: The House of Representatives Magazine*, No. 24, August.

Van Holsteyn, J.O. (2005) '"To Refer or Not to Refer, That's the Question": On the First National Referendum in the Netherlands', paper presented at the ECPR Workshop, Budapest.

Van Onselen, P. and Errington, W. (2004) 'Electoral Databases: Big Brother or Democracy Unbound?', *Australian Journal of Political Science*, Vol. 39, No. 2.

Verba, S, Nie, N.H. and Kim, J. (1978) *Participation and Political Equality*, Chicago, University of Chicago Press.

Walker, David (2001) 'The Party's Over', *Guardian*, 16 January.

Wanna, John (2005) 'The Australian Federal Election 2004: Howard's Scare Campaign Prompted Labor's "Train-Wreck"', *Representation*, Vol. 41, No. 4.

Weaver, R. Kent and Rockman, Bert A. (eds) (1993) *Do Institutions Matter? Government Capabilities in the United States and Abroad*, Washington, DC, Brookings Institution.

Weber, Max (1918) 'Wissenschaft als Beruf', in *Gesammelte politische Schriften*, Tübingen, Mohr.

Weinberg, Leonard L. and Eubank, W.E. (1987) 'Italian Women Terrorists', *Terrorism: An International Journal*, Vol. 9, No. 3.

White, Stephen (2002) *Edmund Burke: Modernity, Politics and Aesthetics*, London, Rowman & Littlefield.

Wilcox, D. (1912) *Government by All the People (or the Initiative, the Referendum and the Recall as Instruments of Democracy)*, New York, Macmillan.

WIHSC (1997) *Report of the Citizens' Jury on Genetic Testing for Common Disorders*, Pontypridd, Welsh Institute for Health and Social Care, University of Glamorgan.

Wilde, O. (1997) *The Soul of Man Under Socialism*, in *The Collected Works of Oscar Wilde*, Ware, Wordsworth Editions .

World Value Survey (1990) www.worldvaluessurvey.org/services/index.html.

Wright, Tony (ed.) (2000) *The British Political Process*, London, Routledge.

Wright, Tony (2003) *British Politics: A Very Short Introduction*, Oxford, Oxford University Press.

Wright, Tony (2004) 'Prospects for Parliamentary Reform', *Parliamentary Affairs*, Vol. 57, No. 4.

Wyller, C. (1996) 'Norway: Six Exceptions to the Rule', in Michael Gallagher and Pier Vincenzo Uleri (eds) *The Referendum Experience in Europe*, London, Macmillan.

Ysmal, C. (2004) 'France', *European Journal of Political Research*, Vol. 43, No. 4.

Index

EU authorised representative for GPSR:
Easy Access System Europe, Mustamäe tee 50,
10621 Tallinn, Estonia
gpsr.requests@easproject.com

www.ingramcontent.com/pod-product-compliance
Lightning Source LLC
Chambersburg PA
CBHW061737270326
41928CB00011B/2264